# DUNDEE FC
*On This Day*

# DUNDEE FC
## *On This Day*

*History, Facts & Figures*
*from Every Day of the Year*

**KENNY ROSS**

# DUNDEE FC
## *On This Day*

### *History, Facts & Figures from Every Day of the Year*

*All statistics, facts and figures are correct as of 1st July 2017*

© Kenny Ross

Kenny Ross has asserted his rights in accordance with the Copyright,
Designs and Patents Act 1988 to be identified as the author of this work.

Published By:
Pitch Publishing (Brighton) Ltd
A2 Yeoman Gate
Yeoman Way
Durrington
BN13 3QZ

Email: info@pitchpublishing.co.uk
Web: www.pitchpublishing.co.uk

Published 2017

A catalogue record for this book is available from the British Library

ISBN 9781785313233

Typesetting and origination by Pitch Publishing
Printed in Great Britain by TJ International

## DEDICATION

For My Mum

For over 50 years she has checked Dundee's
result at 4.45pm to see what mood my Dad
or I might be in.

Thanks for everything.

# FOREWORD

I was delighted to be asked to write the foreword for this book, as Kenny Ross is the most knowledgeable person I know, regarding Dundee FC. I am sure it will be an excellent read.

I signed for the Dark Blues on the 6th January 1961 and my time was short, successful and varied. It included a brief relegation battle, a championship win, reaching the semi-final of the European Cup and a short spell working with the talented young reserve players. In effect, it gave me a golden finish to my footballing career.

Why was the Dens Park club so successful at that time? Because everything was so positive. The first team had special talents with the right balance of youth and experience; the enthusiastic reserve lads were hungry for club success; the backroom staff helped greatly in creating the right spirit in the dressing room and the fans were terrific throughout the spell. But the man who put it all together was the modest manager Bob Shankly. He never received the full credit he deserved nor did he seek it. Football was his life and he just wanted to do his best for the club and he certainly did. He will never be forgotten!

Yes it was undoubtedly a great time to be a Dark Blue in whatever capacity!

*Bobby Wishart (Dundee FC 1961 – 1964)*
*Scottish League championship winner 1961/62*
*European Cup semi-finalist 1962/63*
*Hall of Fame Legends Award 2012*

# INTRODUCTION

*Dundee FC On This Day* follows the ups and downs of the club in the form of facts, figures and trivia for each date of the year since the club was founded in 1893.

2018 will marks the club's 125th anniversary of the club since they were founded with the merger of local sides Our Boys and East End and it has been a dramatic journey. This book charts that journey by starting on January 1st, winding its way out of winter, through the spring, summer and autumn months and into December; the month Dundee last won a major trophy.

There are title winnings, trophy triumphs, derby highs, European football, promotions and of course the incredible Dee-Fiant season, all countered by relegations, cup upsets and two administrations. There have been plenty of terrific players and memorable matches and these memories, both happy and sad, bring to life the colourful history of this wonderful club.

Supporting Dundee Football Club has always been a rollercoaster ride and you can go from the high of the 'Doon Derby' to the low of losing a cup final but if it doesn't end well in May, it all starts again in August. It's actually pretty comforting when you think about it!

# ACKNOWLEDGEMENTS

The author would like to acknowledge the help, support and advice from Tommy Young, David Young, Alasdair Leslie, Derek Gerrard, Jim Davie, Mark Robertson, Jim Mitchell, Norrie Price, Bob Donald, Jim Christie, Claire Scanlon and Dundee's managing director John Nelms. Special thanks has to go to Jim Davie for undertaking the difficult and arduous task of proof reading and to Dundee legend Bobby Wishart for his fantastic foreword. It is an honour to have one of Dundee's 1962 title winning side write it.

The author would like to acknowledge the information in Norrie Price's *Up Wi' the Bonnets* and *They Wore the Dark Blue*, Jim Hendry's *Dundee Greats* and Jim Wilkie's *Across the Great Divide*. These superb books have been an invaluable source of information alongside the newspapers and match programmes of the day.

The author would also like to give a special thanks to club photographers David Young and Derek Gerrard for permission to use their excellent illustrations. Both do a terrific job on a matchday and have an excellent catalogue of images and thanks also goes to John Nelms for permission to use the club logo and pictures.

Dundee have an excellent team behind the scenes at Dens Park who have all helped in some capacity and an excellent media team of which the author is proud to be part and thanks them for their support.

# DUNDEE FC
## *On This Day*

# JANUARY

## MONDAY 1st JANUARY 1894

Dundee's first ever New Year's Day game is a friendly against Newton Heath, the original name of Manchester United. Played in front of 6,000 at Dundee's first ground, West Craigie Park, The Dee win 2-1 thanks to goals from Jimmy Dundas and Bill Thomson.

## TUESDAY 1st JANUARY 1946

A Ne'erday derby at Tannadice sees Dundee defeat Dundee United 3-2 in front of a crowd of 16,000. Goals from Albert Juliussen, Bob Bowman (pen) and Ronnie Turnbull give Dundee victory on the way to winning the Scottish League B Division title, although they would be denied promotion to the top flight as the season was deemed unofficial with players still being demobbed from the army.

## WEDNESDAY 1st JANUARY 1947

Dundee beat Dundee United on New Year's Day for the second year in a row with a 2-0 win at Dens thanks to goals from Ronnie Turnbull and Ernie Ewen. Dundee would go on to win the Scottish League B Division for the second season in succession and this time were granted promotion. Dundee use shirt numbers for the first time with red numbers on dark blue shirts and issue their first ever match programme.

## FRIDAY 1st JANUARY 1988

Dundee bring their game against Dunfermline Athletic forward 24 hours to allow striker Tommy Coyne the chance to grab the Daily Record's 'Goalden Shot' title for the first Scottish League player to score 30 goals. 'The Cobra' scores his 29th and 30th goals of the season to defeat The Pars 2-0 at Dens and pips Ally McCoist to the award as he was due to play in the Old Firm derby the following day.

## MONDAY 2nd JANUARY 1899

Dundee play their last ever game at their second home of Carolina Port with a New Year local derby against Wanderers. 'The Port' has a superb playing surface but it is too remote and has no public transport links, meaning large crowds only really turned out for big games. Even then, hundreds used to get a free view from 'the burning mountain', a smoking slag heap at the adjacent gas works on Broughty Ferry Road. Dundee win the friendly 5-0 with Harry Stewart having the honour of scoring the last goal at the ground.

DERBY DELIGHT! NICK ROSS SLIDES IN FRONT OF THE DUNDEE FANS TO CELEBRATE HIS NEW YEAR WINNER OVER UNITED

## SATURDAY 2nd JANUARY 2016

Dundee beat bottom of the table Dundee United 2-1 at Dens. United take the lead before Japanese debutant goalkeeper Kawashima punches a Nicky Low free kick straight up into the air for Kane Hemmings to volley home the equaliser. Nick Ross' deflected shot from the edge of the box seals a memorable win.

## TUESDAY 3rd JANUARY 1939

A John Lawrie hat-trick helps Dundee to a 4-1 Division Two win over Edinburgh City in the capital. Dundee's top scorer Charlie McGillivray nets Dundee's other counter. City, who played their home games at the Powderhall Stadium, would finish the season in 18th and last place in the Scottish League.

## SATURDAY 4th JANUARY 1964

Dundee defeat Third Lanark 6-0 at Dens in their third game of the New Year with goals from Alan Gilzean (2), Andy Penman, Bobby Waddell, Alan Cousin and Kenny Cameron. Dundee would score an incredible 152 goals in the 1963/64 season with four of the scorers, Gilzean (52), Penman (30), Waddell (20) and Cameron (22) scoring at least 20 each and Cousin scoring 15.

## SATURDAY 4th JANUARY 1975

Dundee win the New Year derby for the third year in a row with a 2-0 win at Dens in front of a 16,184 crowd. Gordon Wallace makes a welcome return from injury and his clever distribution and unselfish running are a major factor in the success. Wallace opens the scoring and Ian Anderson gets the second while centre-half George Stewart ensures United's highly-rated youngster Andy Gray is given little chance to shine.

## SATURDAY 5th JANUARY 1974

Dundee are unbeaten for the whole of January and February and the highlight is the Dark Blues' first win 'across the road' in eight years. A 12,000 crowd turns up at Tannadice for the derby and a John Duncan brace gives Dundee a 2-1 win over Dundee United. It is the second year in a row that Duncan scores a New Year double against The Arabs after scoring twice in the 3-0 win at Dens the previous year.

## FRIDAY 6th JANUARY 1961

Bobby Wishart signs for Dundee from Aberdeen for £3,500. A cultured left-half, Wishart won the Scottish League championship with The Dons in 1955 and would repeat that feat with Dundee in 1962. Wishart would score 14 goals in 108 appearances in three years at Dens and was inducted into the club's Hall of Fame in 2012 with a Legends Award.

## SATURDAY 6th JANUARY 1962

The Dundee v Falkirk match goes ahead despite the Dens Park pitch being close to frozen. Alan Gilzean takes the unusual step of wearing sandshoes to combat the conditions and it is a decision that pays off as Gillie scores twice in a 2-1 win during Dundee's title-winning campaign.

## SATURDAY 7th JANUARY 1961

Bobby Wishart immediately endears himself to the Dundee support on his debut as he scores twice as the Dark Blues defeat Dundee United 3-0 in front of a crowd of 22,000 at Dens. Bobby Adamson rounds off the scoring with his only goal for The Dee.

## WEDNESDAY 8th JANUARY 1930

Hugh Ferguson had scored the only goal in Cardiff's FA Cup Final win over Arsenal in 1927 but his subsequent move to Tayside ends in tragedy. Joining Dundee in the summer of 1929 he does not hit it off at Dens and after just two goals in 17 games, the centre forward, who had been barracked from a section of the home support, finds himself out of the team by December. On the evening of January 8th Ferguson leaves his digs, telling his landlady he is going to the cinema but instead he breaks into Dens Park and gasses himself in the main stand pavilion. As the player had lost form, his self-confidence had drained away and, unknown to anyone, he had suffered a nervous breakdown. He is tragically found dead the following morning.

## SATURDAY 9th JANUARY 1897

Dundee defeat Highland League Inverness Caledonian 7-1 at Dens in the first round of the Scottish Cup. Dave Willocks, who would finish the season as top goalscorer, scores a hat-trick and the win is completed with goals from Jim Smith, Joe Devlin (2) and Jimmy Dundas.

## SATURDAY 10th JANUARY 1998

James Grady scores a hat-trick as Dundee win 5-2 against Ayr United at Somerset Park. Brian Irvine and Steve McCormick also score on The Dee's successful road to the First Division title. Grady would win the First Division Player of the Year at the end of the season though would be beaten to the Dundee Player of the Year by goalkeeper Robert Douglas who would go on to win the Andrew De Vries Memorial Trophy an unprecedented three times in his two spells at the club.

## SATURDAY 11th JANUARY 1930

An Andy Campbell goal is enough to give Dundee a 1-0 win against Dundee United in front of 16,000 at Tannadice. Campbell would have a superb derby record, scoring eight times against United and is Dundee's joint top scorer against their neighbours alongside Jocky Scott. It is Dundee's second league win 'across the road' since United changed their name from Dundee Hibernian in 1923.

## SATURDAY 12th JANUARY 1963

Having been victims of a shock defeat to Fraserburgh in the Scottish Cup four years before, manager Bob Shankly is so concerned about the conditions in Inverness ahead of a first round tie with another Highland League side, Caledonian, that he sneaks out of the team's hotel at midnight and climbs the wall at Telford Street to inspect the pitch. He finds Caley had already cleared the snow to try and get the game on in front of a bumper all ticket crowd, so in view of the rock-hard pitch Shankly duly procured a set of rubber boots for his players in the morning. It worked a treat as Dundee win 5-1 thanks to goals from Andy Penman (2), Hugh Robertson, Alan Gilzean and Alan Cousin.

## SATURDAY 13th JANUARY 1900

Dundee defeat Dumfries and Galloway non-league side Douglas Wanderers 8-0 at Dens Park in the Scottish Cup first round thanks to goals from Fred McDiarmid (2), Tommy Low (2), Sandy Keillor, Alex Robertson (2) and Tommy McDermott.

## SATURDAY 13th JANUARY 1962

Gordon Smith is involved in a car crash travelling from his home in North Berwick to Edinburgh for Dundee's match at Tynecastle but is determined to play against his former club, Heart of Midlothian. Despite being badly shaken, Smith, who would go on at the end of the season to win his fifth championship medal with his third club (after winning the title with Hearts and Hibs), sets up both Dundee goals for Alan Cousin and Alan Gilzean in the 2-0 Dundee win.

## SATURDAY 14th JANUARY 1905

Dundee defeat league leaders Celtic 2-1 in front of 13,000 at Dens thanks to goals from Tom Brown and David Wilson. Celtic would go on to win the first of six consecutive Scottish League Division One titles, while Dundee would finish seventh.

## SATURDAY 15th JANUARY 1916

Two goals from top scorer Davie Brown give Dundee a 2-0 victory over Rangers in front of 11,000 at Dens in Division One. Unlike during the Second World War, matches during the First World War were deemed official by the Scottish League.

## TUESDAY 16th JANUARY 1996

Gary McKeown makes a welcome return from a long term knee injury and a Gerry Britton goal is enough to give Dundee a 1-0 Scottish League First Division win over Clydebank in front of only 603 fans at Kilbowie.

## SATURDAY 17th JANUARY 1931

Dundee set a new club record with a 10-1 home win over Highland League Fraserburgh in the first round of the Scottish Cup. There are doubles for George Dempster, Harry Ritchie and Scotland internationalist Colin McNab while Alec Troup, Willie Blyth, Peter Gavigan and top scorer Andy Campbell complete the scoring.

## WEDNESDAY 17th JANUARY 1962

Dundee were looking for revenge against Aberdeen in a rearranged game, originally postponed on New Year's Day due to snow. Aberdeen are to date the only side to have defeated The Dee in the league that season and Dundee felt aggrieved at Pittodrie with the award of a controversial penalty to The Dons. In one of football's many ironies the same referee, Mr A Crossman from Edinburgh, is in charge of the return fixture and this time awards Dundee a controversial spot kick which wins the game. Alan Cousin opens the scoring before Mulhall equalises before the break and 'The Penalty King' Andy Penman steps up to give Dundee a 2-1 win from 12 yards in the second half.

## SATURDAY 17th JANUARY 2004

Late goals from Nacho Novo and Barry Smith earn Dundee a 2-1 win over Partick Thistle at Firhill in perhaps one of the most important wins in the club's history. The Dark Blues have failed to win a game since going into administration in November and are sliding towards the bottom of the league but the skipper's last minute strike from the edge of the box sparks pandemonium in the away end. It not only gives Dundee their first win in ten games and a nine-point cushion over the last placed Jags but also lifts the beleaguered spirits and proves the fight is well and truly on to save the club.

## SATURDAY 18th JANUARY 1964

After scoring six goals in the previous two weeks against Third Lanark and Forres Mechanics, Dundee defeat East Stirlingshire 5-1 at Firs Park. Alan Cousin and Bobby Waddell both net a brace with Alan Gilzean rounding off the scoring against Division One's bottom side.

## SATURDAY 19th JANUARY 1895

Dundee knock Scottish champions Celtic out the third round of the Scottish Cup with a 1-0 win at Carolina Port. Bill Sawers scored the winning goal in front of 12,000 in one of the shocks of the round. It is the Dark Blues' largest home crowd of the season and a record attendance for Dundee at Carolina Port.

## SATURDAY 20th JANUARY 1894

Dundee win their first ever trophy in their inaugural season when they beat Dundee Harp 4-0 in the Forfarshire Cup final. The final is played in front of 10,000 at Carolina Port which would become Dundee's ground in March and the goals come from Jimmy Dundas (2), Sandy Keillor and Bill Thomson. Later in the year Harp are suspended by the SFA for an inability to pay match guarantees to visiting clubs and soon disappear from the scene.

## TUESDAY 20th JANUARY 1959

Andy Penman signs for Dundee on an amateur contract and makes his debut as a 15-year-old just two weeks later against Hearts at Tynecastle. Nicknamed 'The Penalty King' due to his prowess from 12 yards, Penman is part of the 1962 League Championship winning side and would score 141 goals in 306 appearances for the club. He is inducted into the club's Hall of Fame with a Legends Award in 2011 and there is a hospitality lounge at Dens and a supporters club in his native Fife named in his honour.

## SATURDAY 20th JANUARY 1968

Just 4,500 witness an incredible game at Dens as Dundee defeat Kilmarnock 6-5 thanks to goals from George McLean (2), Billy Campbell (2), Alex Bryce and Alec Stuart. The home fans are certainly getting their money's worth after witnessing 4-3 and 5-4 defeats to Partick and Celtic respectively the previous month.

## SATURDAY 21st JANUARY 1956

Alan Gilzean signs from Coupar Angus Juniors and becomes the greatest goalscorer in the club's history. Gillie is part of the championship winning side in 1962 and holds the club records for top overall scorer (169 goals in 190 competitive games), top scorer in one season (52 goals in 1963/64), top European scorer (9 goals), top scorer in one game (7 goals against Queen of the South in 1962, a record shared with Bert Juliussen), top successive scorer (7 goals in 7 consecutive games - January 1st to February 1st 1964) and top hat-trick scorer (17 hat-tricks). He was inducted into the inaugural Hall of Fame in 2009 with a Legends Award and a lounge at Dens bears his name as does a supporters club based in Blairgowrie near his hometown.

### SATURDAY 22nd JANUARY 1910

Dundee played their first match on the road to winning the Scottish Cup with a 1-1 draw against Beith at Dens Park. The non-league club agreed to 'sell' home advantage and play at Dens and on a frosty surface Jimmy Bellamy missed an early penalty for The Dee before going ahead through George Comrie. Beith fight back to earn a replay which Dundee win thanks to a George Langlands winner.

### SATURDAY 22nd JANUARY 1921

Dundee defeat Highland League Inverness Caledonian 8-1 in the first round of the Scottish Cup in front of 18,000 at Dens. George Phillip scores a hat-trick with Tom Jackson, Alec Troup, Dyken Nicol and Willie McLean also on target.

### SATURDAY 22nd JANUARY 1949

Alec Stott scores four and Johnny Pattillo two as Dundee win 6-1 at home to Scottish League B Division St Johnstone in the first round of Scottish Cup at Dens. Dundee would reach the semi-finals after beating St Mirren after a replay in the next round and then getting a bye in the third.

### SATURDAY 23rd JANUARY 1909

John 'Sailor' Hunter and Jimmy Bellamy both score hat-tricks as Dundee beat Ayr Parkhouse 9-0 at Dens in the Scottish Cup. Two of Bellamy's goals are penalties with Sandy MacFarlane, Herbert Dainty and George Langlands completing the scoring.

### WEDNESDAY 24th JANUARY 1962

Dundee go 20 games undefeated in all competitions with a 2-1 win over St Johnstone at home in their title-winning year in a game originally scheduled for December 30th, postponed due to frost. Alan Gilzean gives Dundee the lead in 22 minutes with an 18-yard strike and McVitie equalises eight minutes later with a similar hit. Alex Ferguson is in Bobby Brown's side who lose 2-1 after Andy Penman gets the winner with 20 minutes left.

## SATURDAY 25th JANUARY 1936

Dundee defeat Babcock Wilcox 6-0 in the Scottish Cup first round in front of only 1,073 fans at Dens. Having recently acquired full SFA membership, the Renfrew engineering works team enter the Scottish Cup through the Qualifying Cup (South) but are dispatched at the first hurdle thanks to goals from Tommy Robertson, Jimmy Guthrie, Archie Coats, Tom Smith and Bobby Adamson (2).

## SATURDAY 25th JANUARY 1947

Scottish League B Division Dundee stun Celtic in the first round of the Scottish Cup with a 2-1 win at Dens. The match caught the imagination of the footballing public with all 36,000 tickets snapped up at prices of 5/- and 3/6d for the stand, 2/6d for the enclosure and 1/6d for the ground with thousands more disappointed. The Dark Blues showed little respect for their A Division opponents and a raging 25-yarder from Ernie Ewen puts them ahead after 15 minutes. Ronnie Turnbull added a second after an hour and although Celtic pulled one back in the dying minutes, The Dee hold on for a famous win.

## SATURDAY 25th JANUARY 1986

Dundee defeat Highland League Nairn County 7-0 away in the Scottish Cup third round. Initially the frozen surface looks as if it might present problems but with the on-song Graham Harvey grabbing a hat-trick and goals from Stuart Rafferty, Rab Shannon (2) and Colin Hendry, the Dark Blues eventually romp to victory.

## MONDAY 25th JANUARY 1988

Dundee win the Tennents Sixes; an annual indoor six-a-side tournament contested by Premier Division clubs between 1984 and 1993. Having topped their group at the SECC in Glasgow the day before with a 9-3 win over Aberdeen and a 2-1 victory over Morton, the Dark Blues then beat Dundee United 4-3 in the quarter-final in the first Monday night match. A 4-1 win over Aberdeen in the semi-final sets up a final with Motherwell which Dundee win 3-2, allowing captain Bobby Geddes to lift the trophy which resides in the Dens Park boardroom today.

## SATURDAY 25th JANUARY 2003

Dundee start their Road to Hampden with a 2-0 win at Partick Thistle at Firhill. Right from the kick off The Dee take control with the rejuvenated Giorgi Nemsadze pulling the strings in midfield and he opens the scoring with a brilliantly curled free kick on the half hour. Nine minutes from time Dundee get the decisive second when Gavin Rae plays a one-two with Nacho Novo before rattling home the rebound after his first effort is blocked.

## SUNDAY 25th JANUARY 2004

'The Monopoly Derby'. Dundee United fans throw monopoly money as Dundee take to the field after The Dee had plunged into administration the previous November but it is the Dark Blues who have the last laugh. Inspired by the energetic Garry Brady, Dundee dominate only for Billy Dodds to put United ahead with a 44th minute penalty after Brent Sancho, an earlier substitute for the injured Lee Wilkie, needlessly downs Charlie Miller. Sancho makes amends when, early in the second half, he hooks the ball back across the goal for Nacho Novo to bundle home from a couple of yards out. Then with 20 minutes left, substitute Steve Lovell beats Wilson with his left foot before brilliantly sweeping the ball past Gallagher with his right to give the Dark Blues a priceless 2-1 win. In front of the live BBC cameras, The Dee show they are down but not out and still fighting!

## SATURDAY 26th JANUARY 1946

Faced with the prospect of just a minimum of 32 League and Cup fixtures, clubs in the Scottish League B Division organise the Supplementary Cup to dovetail the end of the League fixture card in January. In the first round, first leg Dundee defeat Cowdenbeath 4-1 at Central Park thanks to goals from Ronnie Turnbull (2), Tommy Gallacher and Bobby Ancell. A 2-2 draw at Dens a week later sees The Dee through 6-3 on aggregate.

## SATURDAY 27th JANUARY 1990

Dundee defeat Hibernian 2-0 at Dens thanks to goals from Keith Wright and skipper Gordon Chisholm. It is Dundee's first win in ten games in a season in which Dundee would finish bottom of the Premier Division.

## SATURDAY 28th JANUARY 1911

Dundee started off their defence of the Scottish Cup with a 2-1 win over Hibernian in front of 22,000 at Dens Park. Sandy MacFarlane, who would later have two spells as manager in the twenties, scores Dundee's first and R C Hamilton gets the winner.

## SATURDAY 29th JANUARY 1983

Brora Rangers become Dundee's first Highland League visitors in the Scottish Cup for 52 years and give the Dark Blues a scare. Despite Dundee's non-stop attacks on the muddy surface, the Brora part-timers defend gallantly but with just 30 seconds remaining, Eric Sinclair's diving header clinches a 2-1 victory for The Dee.

## SATURDAY 30th JANUARY 1904

Dundee defeat Celtic 2-1 at Dens thanks to goals from Sandy MacFarlane and Dicky Boyle. Dundee would finish fifth and Celtic third with Third Lanark the champions of Scotland for the first and only time in their history, winning the title on the last day at home to Dundee.

## SATURDAY 31st JANUARY 1903

After receiving a 'walkover' against Barholm Rovers in the first round, Dundee defeat Nithsdale Wanderers 7-0 at Dens in the Scottish Cup second round at Dens. Jimmy Dickson and Willie White both score hat-tricks against the side from Sanquhar in Dumfries and Galloway with Tommy Robertson netting the final counter.

## WEDNESDAY 31st JANUARY 1951

Four days after throwing away a 2-0 lead in front of 38,000 at Dens, Dundee cross the road to face B Division Dundee United in a Scottish Cup fourth round replay. Twenty thousand turn up for the afternoon kick-off to witness Dundee superstar Billy Steel score with a swerving 30-yard shot to win the match 1-0. The strike completely deceives United keeper Wylie and the internationalist cheekily claims to the press afterwards that he had intentionally put 'screw' on the ball!

# DUNDEE FC
## *On This Day*

# FEBRUARY

## SATURDAY 1st FEBRUARY 1964

Dundee beat Queen of the South 6-2 in Division One at Dens thanks to goals from Kenny Cameron (2), Alan Gilzean (3) and Andy Penman. Incredibly, it is Dundee's 32nd goal in just five games after wins over Third Lanark (6-0), Forres Mechanics (6-3), East Stirlingshire (5-1) and Brechin City (9-2) in consecutive weeks.

## SATURDAY 2nd FEBRUARY 1991

In front of the *Sportscene* cameras that had come to Dens after a postponement in Perth, Dundee keep up their promotion challenge when they beat Hamilton Academical 3-2 in the First Division. Goals from Colin West (2) and Rab Shannon secure the win and successive victories over Clydebank, Airdrie and Ayr put Dundee back on top of the league.

## SATURDAY 3rd FEBRUARY 1962

After losing their first match in 19 games the week before, in a 1-0 Scottish Cup defeat at home to St Mirren, league leaders Dundee travel to Rugby Park and draw 1-1 with Kilmarnock. Kerr gives the hosts the lead just after the hour but Alan Cousin keeps Dundee's title challenge on track with an 88th minute equaliser from close range.

## TUESDAY 3rd FEBRUARY 2004

Livingston joined Dundee in administration 48 hours before the sides met in the League Cup semi-final at Easter Road. In a tight game Dundee looked the more likely to score as the game moved towards extra time but with just 60 seconds left, Lee Mair and Brent Sancho allow a speculative ball to bounce through and as Julian Speroni hesitates, Pasquinelli goes down in a tussle with Mair. Referee Mike McCurry awards a penalty and Derek Lilley steps up to fire home the winner.

## WEDNESDAY 4th FEBRUARY 1987

Tommy Coyne joined Dundee from Dundee United for £75,000 in December but had to wait until February for his first Dark Blue goal. Dundee met First Division East Fife in the Scottish Cup at Dens after an earlier postponement due to a waterlogged pitch and had to rely on a late Tommy Coyne goal to earn a 2-2 draw. Having scored his first goal for the club, Coyne scores his second three days later in the league at Clydebank and his third two days after that in the 4-1 replay win at Bayview. Coyne would go on to become a Dundee legend, scoring 60 goals in 127 appearances and would be inducted into the club's Hall of Fame in 2011 with a Legends Award.

### SATURDAY 5th FEBRUARY 1938

Dundee had lost 6-0 to Rangers at Ibrox earlier in the season but gain some astonishing revenge with a 6-1 win in front of 15,000 at Dens in the return fixture. Venters puts Rangers ahead against the run of play on 18 minutes but playing down the slope, with a strong wind behind them, Dundee hit back strongly with doubles from Arthur Baxter and Archie Coats to give them a 4-1 half time lead. Baxter completes his hat-trick on 83 minutes after a Coats header rebounds off the post and Jimmy Boyd sends the Dens fans home in raptures when he makes it 6-1 with two minutes remaining.

### TUESDAY 5th FEBRUARY 1963

A harsh winter decimated the football programme from early January and Dundee managed only two competitive games in two months, both Scottish Cup ties. In The Dee's only match in February they defeat Montrose 8-0 at Dens in the second round thanks to goals from Alan Cousin (2), Alan Gilzean (2), Bobby Wishart, Hugh Robertson, Bobby Waddell and Gordon Smith.

### SATURDAY 5th FEBRUARY 2011

Having been hit with a draconian 25-point penalty by the Scottish League for going into administration for a second time, Dundee are bottom of the First Division but after a remarkable 13-game unbeaten league run they move out of last place for the first time with a 2-1 win away at Queen of the South. The home side had the majority of the pressure and squandered a number of chances but it is Dundee who took the lead on 35 minutes when Craig Forsyth drilled home a right-footed shot at the back post. Dundee continued to defend stoutly into the second half but their luck ran out on the hour when Ryan McGuffie equalised with a header to score the first goal against The Dee in just over 12 hours. Dundee however got the winner when in a rare breakaway up field, Nicky Riley wins a header at the edge of the box and as it falls to Sean Higgins, he turns to volley home an overhead kick to score his first goal since October and give Dundee the lead. The goal seems to settle Dundee and the game is seen out with relative ease although it still takes a spectacular save from Robert Douglas late on to ensure the three points and move Dundee into ninth.

### SATURDAY 6th FEBRUARY 2010

Dundee defeat Ayr United 2-1 in the Scottish Cup at Dens thanks to goals from on-loan Celtic striker Ben Hutchinson and future Celtic striker Leigh Griffiths.

### SATURDAY 7th FEBRUARY 1925

Dundee knocked Scottish League Third Division side Lochgelly United out of the Scottish Cup en route to the final. Goals from Charlie Duncan and Willie Rankine send 'The Happylanders' back across the Tay to Fife with a 2-1 defeat.

### WEDNESDAY 8th FEBRUARY 1928

After a 3-3 draw at Tannadice with Dundee United four days earlier, Dundee knock their lower league neighbours out of the Scottish Cup with a 1-0 win at Dens in the second round replay, thanks to a Willie O'Hare winner.

### WEDNESDAY 8th FEBRUARY 1956

Four days previous Dundee's Scottish Cup campaign begins with a 2-2 draw at a snow covered Tannadice but in the Wednesday afternoon replay, Dundee made no mistake against Division Two Dundee United with a comfortable 3-0 win. The derby is won by goals from George Merchant, Ian Stables and Albert Henderson.

### WEDNESDAY 8th FEBRUARY 1961

Dundee defeat league leaders Rangers 4-2 in front of 22,000 at Dens with goals from Bobby Wishart, Alan Cousin and Alan Gilzean (2). The Dark Blues can't repeat the victory in the Scottish Cup seven days later when Rangers return to 'Juteopolis' to win 5-1 in front of 10,000 more fans.

## SATURDAY 8th FEBRUARY 2014

The top two in the SPFL Championship, Dundee and Hamilton, were due to meet at Dens on January 18th but the match was postponed at 1.45pm due to a waterlogged pitch. By the time the match is rearranged two weeks later, when both clubs have a free weekend due to early exits from the Scottish Cup, Dundee have a new manager after John Brown resigns in the wake of a 2-0 defeat at Falkirk and a 1-1 draw with Alloa in the interim. Paul Hartley is appointed as Dundee manager on February 5th and takes charge of his first match against one of his former clubs three days later and gets Dundee's promotion challenge back on track with a 1-0 win over the Accies thanks to a Martin Boyle winner.

## SATURDAY 9th FEBRUARY 1952

Dundee travel to non-league Wigtown & Bladnoch in the second round of the Scottish Cup and despite a population of just 1,300 and admission prices of 2s, double the usual charge for South of Scotland matches, a bumper crowd of 4,500 attend. Billy Steel opens the scoring in ten minutes but Wigtown get a chance to live their dream when they equalise on 28 minutes through inside-left Cowan. Trammondford Park goes crazy but their joy is short-lived when Johnny Pattillo restores Dundee's lead just two minutes later. Steel gets his second before George Hill makes it 4-1 before half-time and Wigtown's dream is well and truly shattered. Dundee don't let up in the second half where further scores from Pattillo and Hill and a goal from George Christie give The Dee a comfortable 7-1 win.

## SATURDAY 9th FEBRUARY 1966

Dundee's Scottish Cup tie with East Fife is initially postponed due to a flu epidemic amongst the Dark Blues' squad and goes ahead the following week after two inches of snow is cleared from Dens. Bobby Cox opens the scoring with one of only three goals he would score in his 434 appearances and further goals from Andy Penman (3), Jim McLean (2), Alec Stuart (2) and Kenny Cameron give Dundee a convincing 9-1 win.

## SATURDAY 9th FEBRUARY 1985

Dundee beat Celtic 2-0 in front of 12,087 at Dens thanks to goals from Ray Stephen and a Robert Connor penalty. Dundee can't replicate the win the following month when Celtic win 2-1 at Parkhead in a Scottish Cup quarter-final replay but to get there, the Dark Blues make it an Old Firm double the following week when they knock Rangers out of the Scottish Cup 1-0 at Ibrox thanks to a John Brown winner.

## SATURDAY 10th FEBRUARY 1894

Dundee achieved their biggest win of their inaugural season with an 8-1 victory over Renton at home at West Craigie Park. A 4,000 crowd were treated to goals from top scorer Jimmy Dundas, Sandy Keillor (3), Davie McInroy, Billy Matthew, Sandy Gilligan and Bill Thomson. Renton would finish bottom of the ten-team league with just four points from a win and two draws. Dundee would finish two places ahead of them with 15 points from six wins and three draws.

## SUNDAY 10th FEBRUARY 1974

The continuing energy crisis and the resultant three day week brought the introduction of Sunday football. After defeating Partick Thistle 4-1 at Dens the week before, Dundee travelled to Glasgow and win 2-1 at Celtic Park thanks to goals from Duncan Lambie and John Duncan.

## MONDAY 11th FEBRUARY 2008

First Division Dundee knocked SPL Motherwell out of the Scottish Cup with a spirited victory at Fir Park despite finishing the match with just nine men. After a poor first half, Dundee take the lead on 49 minutes when Paul McHale lashes in a shot from close range and just six minutes later, Scott Robertson pokes the ball home from three yards after a fast break by Kevin McDonald. Darren Smith heads a goal for Well, but Dundee hold on for a 2-1 win to send them into the quarter-finals despite red cards for McDonald and Gary MacKenzie.

DEE-FIANT! NEIL McCANN CELEBRATES HIS FAMOUS 94TH MINUTE WINNER AGAINST RAITH ROVERS

## SATURDAY 12th FEBRUARY 2011

In one of the great Dens Park moments Neil McCann comes out of retirement to score an injury-time winner in a 2-1 victory over Raith Rovers in the Dee-Fiant season. Dundee are unbeaten in 13 league matches but Grant Murray's header on 50 minutes looks like ending that run. Seven minutes later the tide begins to turn when trialist McCann comes off the bench to replace on loan Johnny Stewart. Raith sit back and, with just four minutes left, pay the ultimate price when Dundee win a free kick 30 yards out after McCann is brought down and captain Gary Harkins steps up to bend a beautiful free kick over the wall and high into the top corner to send the stadium wild. The home fans celebrate ecstatically and urge their Dee-Fiant heroes on for the winner and in the fourth minute of injury time, Harkins wins a corner. When the corner comes in, it is cleared by a Raith defender but when it falls to Matt Lockwood outside the box he lofts it back in where it is met by Forsyth who heads the ball down. It lands at the feet of McCann 12 yards out and as he spins and falls to the ground he lifts the ball gently into the air and watches it float over the Rovers keeper and into the net in a moment no Dee who was there will ever forget.

## SATURDAY 13th FEBRUARY 1965

Dundee win 4-1 at Rugby Park thanks to goals from Charlie Cooke (2), Steve Murray and Hugh Robertson. Kilmarnock would ultimately go on to win the League title on goal average from Hearts with a little help from The Dee who win 7-1 at Tynecastle two weeks later.

## SATURDAY 14th FEBRUARY 2015

Fan favourite Paul McGowan scores his first goal for Dundee in the 90th minute in a 1-0 win over Partick Thistle at Dens to keep the Dark Blues on track for a top six finish in their first season back in the top flight.

## SATURDAY 15th FEBRUARY 1964

Dundee beat Forfar Athletic 6-1 at Dens in the Scottish Cup en route to the final thanks to goals from Bobby Wadell (2), Alan Gilzean (2), Alan Cousin and Kenny Cameron. Gilzean's second goal was his 40th of the season, one more than Alex Stott's record of 39 in season 1948/49 and he would finish the season with an astonishing 52 goals.

## SATURDAY 16th FEBRUARY 1895

Dundee draw 1-1 with Renton at Carolina Port in their first ever Scottish Cup semi-final. Semis were played either home or away at this time although the replays were played on neutral venues. A week later Dundee would draw 3-3 with Renton in front of 20,000 at Hampden before losing 3-0 in front of 29,000 at Celtic Park a fortnight later. The West Dunbartonshire side would lose 2-1 to St Bernards in the final at Ibrox.

## SATURDAY 17th FEBRUARY 1945

Dundee defeat Rangers 5-2 at Ibrox in the Scottish League North-East Division. Dundee returned from abeyance in August 1944 while football was organised in 'unofficial' regional basis and goals from Ronnie Turnbull (2), Andy McCall, a Woodburn own goal and Ernie Ewen give the Dark Blues their third win of the season over Rangers.

## SATURDAY 17th FEBRUARY 1962

Having been knocked out of the Scottish Cup by St Mirren in January, on the next cup weekend Dundee arrange a friendly against Arsenal who themselves had exited the FA Cup at the hands of Manchester United. In front of 14,000 at Dens the sides draw 2-2 with the Dark Blues goals coming from Alan Cousin and Alan Gilzean. They would meet again in London on March 10th with The Gunners winning 1-0 in front of a 10,000 crowd at Highbury.

## SUNDAY 17th FEBRUARY 1974

The popularity of Sunday football had brought a 50% increase in gates in Scotland and after 40,000 turn up for Dundee's visit to Parkhead the week before, 65,000 are there for part two of Dundee's Old Firm double header in Glasgow. In a Scottish Cup fourth round tie with Rangers, Jocky Scott opens the scoring five minutes after half time. Rangers have no answer to Dundee's slick passing movements and a double from John Duncan gives The Dee a memorable 3-0 win.

## SATURDAY 18th FEBRUARY 1939

Dundee defeat Stirling side Kings Park 3-0 in front of just 2,000 at Dens in the Scottish League Division Two thanks to goals from Archie Coats, Johnston Melville and Bobby Wilson. Having been relegated the previous year Dundee would finish a disappointing sixth, meaning they would resume in the second tier after the Second World War.

### SATURDAY 19th FEBRUARY 1898

Barring Dundee's way to their first ever Scottish Cup final are Division Two leaders Kilmarnock whom they would meet at Rugby Park before semis were played at a neutral venue. Malcolm McVean puts Dundee ahead in five minutes and gets a second when an attempted clearance by the Killie keeper strikes John Malloch and rebounds into the net. The Ayrshire side are undeterred and pull one back before half-time before going on to win 3-2. Killie would lose 2-0 to Rangers at Hampden in their first ever final.

### SATURDAY 19th FEBRUARY 2011

After his heroics against Raith the previous week, Neil McCann plays his second trialist game, this time from the start against Stirling Albion at the Doubletree Dunblane Stadium. Dundee were vying with Stirling to avoid bottom spot after their 25-point deduction and it turns out to be a difficult afternoon for The Dee. Stirling show plenty of grit and determination and the task is made even harder when Gary Irvine is given a straight red card for a two-footed challenge on Albion's Ross Forsyth with half an hour to go. By then Dundee are 1-0 ahead thanks to Sean Higgins' first half goal and the ten men are able to hold on for a vital three points despite the Dark Blues' seventh red card of the season.

### SUNDAY 19th FEBRUARY 2017

A fantastic team performance brought Dundee a richly deserved 2-1 win against Rangers at Dens Park, their first home win over the Light Blues in 25 years. Mark O'Hara and Kevin Holt put The Dee two goals ahead at half time and although Joe Garner pulled a goal back for caretaker manager Graeme Murty's Rangers, the Dark Blues had the better of the second half and finished the match as the stronger team.

### SATURDAY 20th FEBRUARY 1897

Dundee defeat Celtic 1-0 at Parkhead in the last game of the season. The winner comes from right-winger Joe Clark and The Dee would finish fifth with Celtic two points ahead of them in fourth.

KEVIN HOLT IS MOBBED BY HIS TEAM MATES TO ACCLAIM HIS WINNER AGAINST RANGERS

## SATURDAY 21st FEBRUARY 1925

On the way to the final Dundee beat Airdrieonians 3-1 in front of 22,373 at Dens in the Scottish Cup third round. Goals from Davie McLean, Charlie Duncan and top scorer Davie Halliday, who would finish the season with 24 goals, are enough to see The Dee through.

## SATURDAY 22nd FEBRUARY 2003

The Dark Blues had only beaten The Dons twice at Dens since 1975 but in the Scottish Cup fourth round defeat Aberdeen 2-0 at home en route to the final. The goals came from Nacho Novo and Steve Lovell but the headlines belonged to goalkeeper Julian Speroni who is immense and makes a save that Dons manager Steve Paterson describes as 'one of the best saves I've ever seen' on the television highlights at night. With the score at 1-0 on the half hour, Aberdeen were awarded a free kick just outside the box. Frenchman Eric Deloumeaux took the kick and when it takes a wicked deflection off the wall, it looks a goal all the way. Speroni has other ideas and when he starts moving to his right, he somehow manages to twist in mid air and stretch his arm out to the left to make the stop to keep The Dee ahead and eventually go on to win the match.

## SATURDAY 23rd FEBRUARY 1918

In the summer of 1917 Dundee had been asked by the Scottish League to withdraw from Division One to minimise on travelling for their predominantly west coast opponents and are placed in the recently created Eastern Division. It means Dundee would meet city neighbours Dundee Hibernian in the first competitive derbies and win 2-1 at Tannadice on the way to winning the title thanks to goals from Jim Heron and Tommy Taylor.

## SATURDAY 23rd FEBRUARY 2008

Mickael Antoine-Curier scores a double as promotion-chasing Dundee destroy dismal Stirling Albion at Forthbank. The striker, on loan from Hibs, side-foots home the opener and Colin McMenamin scores on the rebound after goalkeeper Myles Hogarth denies Gavin Swankie. That is followed by a Laurie Ellis own goal and an Antoine-Curier header after the break, then Bob Davidson fires home after a fine dribble. Derek Lyle headed the sixth after Colin Cramb's reply for the bottom side.

## SATURDAY 24th FEBRUARY 1894

West Craigie Park plays host to its last game as the home of Dundee FC when they draw 1-1 with Third Lanark in front of a crowd of 3,000. Top scorer Jimmy Dundas scores the goal in the penultimate game of the Scottish League Division One season with The Dee finishing eighth in their inaugural season.

## SATURDAY 24th FEBRUARY 1973

Dundee beat Stranraer 9-2 at Stair Park in the Scottish Cup fourth round thanks to goals from John Duncan (4), Gordon Wallace (3), Doug Houston and Iain Scott. Both goalscorers Duncan and Wallace would be inducted into the club's Hall of Fame with Legends Awards in 2015 and 2010 respectively.

## SATURDAY 25th FEBRUARY 1939

Dundee beat Leith Athletic 7-0 at Dens in the Scottish League Division Two with the goals coming from Charlie McGillivray, Bob Ramsey (2), Archie Coats (2), Bobby Wilson and Harry Sneddon. McGillivray would finish the season with 29 goals while Coats would score 158 goals in his Dark Blue career and is second only to Alan Gilzean as Dundee's all time top goalscorer.

## SATURDAY 26th FEBRUARY 1938

Dundee defeat St Johnstone 6-1 at Dens thanks to goals from Archie Coats, Harry McMenemy (2), Arthur Baxter (2) and John Laurie. It doesn't prevent Dundee from being relegated in 19th place two months later.

## SATURDAY 27th FEBRUARY 1965

Andy Penman and Kenny Cameron score hat-tricks as Dundee beat Heart of Midlothian 7-1 at Tynecastle. Alan Cousin scores the other goal and the margin of the result would do serious damage to Hearts' title aspirations as they would finish as runners-up to Kilmarnock and lose the league on goal average. If Hearts had conceded two goals less then they would have pipped Killie to the league championship.

## SATURDAY 28th FEBRUARY 1987

Dundee stunned Celtic with a 4-1 win at Dens. Manager Jocky Scott's tactics of playing Bobby Glennie, Jim Smith and Jim Duffy at the back with full backs Stewart Forsyth and Tosh McKinlay pushing into midfield pays dividends. Goals from the much maligned Vince Mennie, Rab Shannon, John Brown and Ross Jack give The Dee a resounding win against the defending champions.

## SATURDAY 29th FEBRUARY 1964

Dundee beat St Mirren 9-2 at Dens thanks to goals from Alan Gilzean (3), Bobby Waddell (2), Alan Cousin, Kenny Cameron (2) and Andy Penman. In January 1965 a bribes case which involved a number of top British players such as England internationals Peter Swan and Tony Kay resulted in St Mirren goalkeeper Dick Beattie being jailed for taking payment to 'throw' games. Although it was Dundee's 5-1 home win over St Mirren the previous season which featured in the prosecution evidence, Beattie makes some spectacular blunders in the 9-2 game although there is no denying the deadliness of Gilzean who scores his fifth hat-trick of the season.

# DUNDEE FC
## *On This Day*

# MARCH

### SATURDAY 1st MARCH 2014

Christian Nade scores his first goal for Dundee as the SPFL Championship leaders maintain their one-point advantage at the top with a 2-0 victory over Greenock Morton. The former Hearts striker gets on the end of Martin Boyle's cross to head the hosts in front. Dundee continue to ask questions of the league's basement side but are often foiled by keeper Derek Gaston before top goalscorer Peter MacDonald doubles the Dark Blues' lead late on when he drills home.

### WEDNESDAY 2nd MARCH 1977

First Division Dundee knock Aberdeen out of the Scottish Cup in the fourth round at Pittodrie. After a 1-1 draw at Dens, Bobby Hutchinson heads Dundee into the lead early in the replay before Duncan Davidson draws the Dons level shortly after the break. With 14 minutes remaining, Willie Miller is short with a back pass to Bobby Clark and the ever alert Hutchinson nips in to net the winner.

### WEDNESDAY 2nd MARCH 1983

With Dundee struggling at the wrong end of the table, an Albert Kidd goal gives The Dee a 1-0 win over Rangers at Dens and a boost to their survival hopes. Dundee would finish the season undefeated to the Light Blues with two draws at Ibrox and two wins at Dens.

### MONDAY 2nd MARCH 1987

Dens Park is chosen as the venue, after the toss of a coin, for the second replay against Meadowbank Thistle in the fourth round of the Scottish Cup and a Tommy Coyne double, his second a penalty, finally knocks the Edinburgh side out at the third attempt. Alan Lawrence had been a thorn in Dundee's side throughout the three games and manager Jocky Scott would pay £35,000 to sign the winger in the aftermath.

### SATURDAY 3rd MARCH 1979

The previous week sees St Mirren defeat Dundee United 4-1 at Tannadice in the Premier League but when they come to First Division Dens on Scottish Cup duty, they are sent back to Paisley with 4-1 fourth round defeat after goals from Alan Lamb, Eric Sinclair (2) and a Billy Pirie penalty.

## SATURDAY 3rd MARCH 2001

Goals from Gavin Rae, Juan Sara and Javier Artero earn Ivano Bonetti's Tayzurri a 3-2 win over St Johnstone in Perth as they chase a top six spot in the first SPL split. Italian defender Marco de Marchi does well at left-back after returning from injury but in the next match against Hearts in the Scottish Cup at Dens four days later, he is sent off for kicking Lee Makel in retaliation and never plays for the club again after being blamed by Bonetti for the 1-0 defeat.

## SATURDAY 4th MARCH 1939

Dundee defeat East Stirlingshire 5-3 at Firs Park in the Scottish League Division Two thanks to a hat-trick from Archie Coats and a double from Charlie McGillivray. The Shire had beaten Dundee 6-5 at Dens the previous October and would concede 130 goals as they finish second bottom the following month.

## SATURDAY 5th MARCH 1949

A noisy crowd of 37,356 watch Hearts and Dundee produce a classic Scottish Cup quarter-final tie in the mud at Tynecastle. The teams go in 2-2 at the break after Ally Gunn and George Hill score for Dundee before Syd Gerrie gives Dundee the lead soon after the restart. The game hangs in the balance until near the end when Hearts are awarded a penalty. Reuben Bennett, who would later become part of Bill Shankly's famous boot room coaching staff at Liverpool, makes a splendid save and soon afterwards Johnny Pattillo makes it 4-2 to clinch matters for The Dee.

## WEDNESDAY 6th MARCH 1963

Dundee defeat Anderlecht 4-1 in Brussels in the European Cup quarter-final first leg in an enthralling tie. Within 60 seconds of the start, the 60,000 Heysel Stadium crowd (the largest attendance ever for a football match in Belgium) are stunned when Alan Gilzean puts Dundee ahead from a pinpoint Gordon Smith cross. In 20 minutes Gilzean scores again with a shot from the edge of the box before Anderlecht pull one back from the spot through Lippens, nine minutes from the break. Just after half time Alan Cousin makes it 3-1 to Dundee. Although Bert Slater performs heroics in the Dundee goal, Gordon Smith shatters the Belgians with a decisive fourth 19 minutes from time. Dundee received a standing ovation from the home crowd at full time.

## SATURDAY 7th MARCH 1903

After a dour 0-0 struggle with Hearts at Dens the week before in the Scottish Cup semi-final, the sides meet again in the replay at Tynecastle and a late goal from Porteous ends Dundee's dream of Scottish Cup glory. Dundee would also finish as runners-up in the league behind champions Hibernian.

## SATURDAY 8th MARCH 1947

Dundee set a new club record win with a 10-0 victory over Alloa Athletic at a muddy Recreation Park. English forward Albert Juliussen, who has recently been the subject of £9,000 bids from both Motherwell and Everton, scores six. The other goals come from Ally Gunn, Peter Rattray, Reggie Smith (who would later become manager George Anderson's number two) and Ernie Ewen.

## SATURDAY 8th MARCH 1952

Dens Park is a 41,000 sell-out for a Scottish Cup quarter-final tie with Aberdeen. South African Ken Ziesing gets the League Cup holders' opener with a tremendous shot before Billy Steel dribbles through the Dons defence for Dundee's second just after the break. Further goals from captain Alfie Boyd from the spot and Steel again emphasises the Dark Blues' superiority as they stroll into the last four.

## TUESDAY 8th MARCH 2011

Dundee equal the 1962 League championship winning side's 19 league game unbeaten record with a 3-1 win away at Cowdenbeath. Dundee go ahead thanks to a Sean Higgins first half goal and extend their advantage just two minutes into the second half through a Matt Lockwood penalty, his fourth of the campaign. Greg Stewart gives the home fans a glimmer of hope six minutes later, but Craig Forsyth puts the game to bed with a headed goal shortly before the end to seal a comprehensive victory and increase the lead over bottom club Stirling Albion to 13 points.

## THURSDAY 9th MARCH 2006

In front of the live Sky Sports cameras, Dundee meet Hamilton Academical in a Scottish Cup quarter-final replay in front of 7,460 at Dens after a 0-0 draw at New Douglas Park. Bobby Mann heads the opener 11 minutes after half-time before Simon Lynch made it 2-0 with a flashing header from a Tam McManus cross. However, for the third time that term, The Dee let a two-goal lead slip, but in extra time substitute Steven Craig, on for Bryan Deasley, breaks through to rifle the ball home and fire Dundee into the semi-final.

## SATURDAY 10th MARCH 1928

A double each from Frank Townrow and Gus Smith gives Dundee a 4-1 win over Hibernian in front of 4,000 fans at Dens. It is Dundee's last home league win of the season with defeats to Raith (1-2) and Rangers (0-1) in the final two games.

## WEDNESDAY 11th MARCH 1964

After a 1-1 draw in front of 30,443 at Dens Park four days earlier, Dundee defeat Motherwell 4-2 at Fir Park in the Scottish Cup quarter-final replay. Goals from Kenny Cameron (2), Alan Gilzean and Bobby Waddell send Dundee into the last four en route to the final.

## WEDNESDAY 12th MARCH 1975

Four days after a last gasp Gordon Wallace header earns Dundee a 1-1 draw with Hearts at Tynecastle, the sides meet again in a Scottish Cup quarter-final replay at Dens. The 22,197 crowd have to wait half an hour for George Stewart to head Dundee into the lead from a corner. Two minutes later Wilson Hoggan outpaces the Hearts defence for Bobby Hutchinson to add a second. By the interval the Jam Tarts are level thanks to a Ralph Callaghan penalty and a Drew Busby header. After half-time the play rages from end to end, but in 59 minutes Gordon Wallace springs the offside trap and Bobby Robinson volleys home the decisive goal.

## SATURDAY 12th MARCH 1977

In the Scottish Cup quarter-final, Dundee meet Arbroath before a 9,558 all-ticket crowd at Gayfield but there is a shock for the large travelling support when The Lichties take a first minute lead. Following a mazy dribble, Gordon Strachan equalises in the 25th minute before a late headed double by substitute Eric Sinclair ensures Dundee's place in the last four with a 3-1 win.

## SATURDAY 12th MARCH 2011

Despite a flurry of snow in the morning, the Dundee v Queen of the South game goes ahead in front of 4,242 eager fans who are treated to a magnificent match. The Dark Blues serve up a feast of football as they come from behind to beat The Doonhamers 2-1 and in the process set a new club record of 20 games undefeated in the league, surpassing the 1962 League championship winning side's record of 19. Ex-Dee Colin McMenamin gives QOS a first-half lead after 30 minutes and his lack of celebration is striking, as he shrugs off his team mates and jogs back to the halfway line. It stays like that until the 65th minute when the best move of the match results in Sean Higgins curling the ball home from the edge of the box to put Dundee level. Bizarrely, club secretary Laura Hayes claims an assist for the goal that makes sure the record is broken. Higgins, who had been struggling badly with a foot injury, is told by Neil McCann, who himself had returned to the side for his third game as a trialist, that when he had played for Rangers some players with similar injuries had wrapped a steak around their injury and played with it inside their boot. Laura walks up Main Street and pays £1.49 out of her own pocket for a minute steak from Yorkes of Dundee butchers and Sean celebrates his goal by mimicking eating his foot with a knife and fork. From that moment on there is only one team in the match and with Dundee hungry for more they push forward and get their reward when Steven O'Donnell's peach of a shot crashes off the underside of the bar and Craig Forsyth reacts first to head home the winner.

## WEDNESDAY 13th MARCH 1963

Dundee defeat Anderlecht 2-1 in the European Cup quarter-final second leg in front of a sell-out 40,000 crowd at Dens. The Belgian champions dominate the opening period and take the lead on the half hour through 'Dynamite' Jack Stockman. Dundee grow stronger on the muddy pitch after the break and their pressure finally pays off when Alan Cousin equalises on 78 minutes before Gordon Smith sweeps home the winner from just inside the box for a 6-2 aggregate win over Real Madrid's conquerors.

## WEDNESDAY 14th MARCH 1962

After a run of four defeats, Dundee stopped the rot with a crucial 0-0 draw against rivals Rangers in front of 35,000 at Dens; the biggest home attendance of the title-winning campaign. Alan Gilzean is out with flu while Rangers fail to have Jim Baxter released from an Army v Navy match in Aldershot and although it is Dundee's seventh game without a win, it prevents Rangers pulling five points clear and renews hope of a first ever championship.

## WEDNESDAY 14th MARCH 2001

A Claudio Caniggia inspired performance of verve and dynamism stuns defending champions Rangers at Ibrox. On 14 minutes the long haired Argentinian despatches a powerful shot in off the near post and a flashing injury time header by Stevie Milne secures the 2-0 win. Rangers liked what they saw of the 34-year-old World Cup superstar and signed Caniggia in May for a £900,000 fee.

## SATURDAY 15th MARCH 1986

Dundee and Rangers are competing for the final Uefa Cup place and the Dark Blues give their chances a boost with a 2-1 win over the Light Blues at Dens. A John Brown penalty winner follows a Graham Harvey goal to give The Dee their second home win over Rangers that season.

## TUESDAY 15th MARCH 1988

After a 0-0 draw with Dundee United at Dens in the Scottish Cup quarter-finals, the sides produce a thriller at Tannadice in the replay three days later. A brilliantly taken double by Eamonn Bannon leaves The Dee two behind at half time and with Tosh McKinlay stretchered off with a broken ankle after a shocking tackle by Kevin Gallagher, things look bleak for Dundee. However, McKinlay's replacement Graham Harvey comes on to play a key role and nets twice to bring the scores level. With seven minutes remaining Harvey is denied a sensational hat-trick when his overhead kick is ruled out for offside. The Dundee fans remember this as 'the hat-trick that never was.' Throughout extra time play rages from end to end but with Tom Carson in the Dundee goal making some breathtaking saves, most memorably tipping a John Clark piledriver over the bar, there is no further score.

## SATURDAY 16th MARCH 1946

In the inaugural Scottish League Cup competition, Dundee defeat Stirling Albion 8-1 in a sectional tie at Dens. Goals from Sammy Cox (2), Albert Juliussen (3), Ronnie Turnbull, and Kinnaird Ouchterlonie (2) gave The Dee revenge for the 2-0 defeat at Annfield and sees them top a section that includes Arbroath before losing 3-1 to Rangers at Hampden in the quarter-final.

## SATURDAY 17th MARCH 1894

Dundee FC took over the financially struggling Athletics Grounds Company, holders of the lease with the Dundee Harbour Trustees and acquired Carolina Port. Strathmore lose their home ground and amalgamate with Johnstone Wanderers as 'the ten bobbers' (Dundee's early nickname was 'the ten-bobbers' as they initially only paid players a modest 10/- per week with a bonus of 2/6d per point) moved into Carolina Port. With the league campaign completed, Dundee play a side called Dundonians in a friendly at their new ground on March 30th and beat their local rivals 6-0. Sandy Gilligan, who scored the first goal at West Craigie Park, has the honour of scoring the first Dundee goal at Carolina Port.

## SATURDAY 17th MARCH 1962

Dundee win their first match in eight to get their title challenge back on track after surviving two first half Raith Rovers penalty claims when the ball strikes Ian Ure's arm on both occasions. Raith do twice take the lead with Alan Cousin first equalising in 13 minutes. In the second half Dundee subject the Kirkcaldy side to an aerial bombardment and it pays dividends when Andy Penman heads home two crosses from Hugh Robertson and Gordon Smith.

## SATURDAY 17th MARCH 1984

After a 2-2 draw at Dens, Dundee travel to Ibrox to take on Rangers in a Scottish Cup quarter-final replay with Glennie, McGeachie and McKinlay missing the tie through suspension. Jim Smith heads Dundee into the lead and then, on 63 minutes, Iain Ferguson finishes off a brilliant three-man move for the Dark Blues' second. Things look bleak for the hosts when former Dee Ian Redford is sent off but McClelland and McPherson level the scores with ten minutes

JOCKY SCOTT OPENS THE SCORING AGAINST HIBS IN THE SCOTTISH CUP IN FRONT OF 28,236 AT EASTER ROAD

remaining. Three minutes later Ferguson crashes a high shot past Nicky Walker to give Dundee a sensational 3-2 win, send them into the semis and end Rangers 21-game unbeaten run.

## MONDAY 18th MARCH 1963

After one of the coldest winters on record in the UK, a fixture backlog means Dundee meet Hibernian in the third round of the Scottish Cup at Dens on a Monday night, two days after a 2-1 home win over Partick. Alan Gilzean missed the Thistle game after a foot wound picked up in Brussels and returns to head the winner in front of a crowd of 16,000.

## MONDAY 18th MARCH 1974

After an electrifying 3-3 draw with Hibs at Easter Road in the Scottish Cup quarter-final, 30,881 turn up for the replay at Dens, rearranged for a Monday night due to an earlier postponement because of a waterlogged pitch. There are long queues at every turnstile, with many not able to gain admission until half time, but by then the game is all but over. Deadly finishing by Jocky Scott (25 minutes), John Duncan (31 minutes) and then Bobby Wilson (40 minutes) gives Dundee a 3-0 lead at the break and there is no further scoring in the second half.

## SATURDAY 19th MARCH 1983

Brian Scrimgeour, who had been forced to play in goal for 85 minutes against Dundee United at Tannadice the previous week when Bobby Geddes was stretchered off, is now restored to midfield and scores the winner against second placed Celtic at Dens. Albert Kidd nets Dundee's opener in the 2-1 win to help earn The Dee an Old Firm double in March.

## SATURDAY 19th MARCH 2011

Dee-Fiant Dundee come from 2-0 down at the Falkirk Stadium to draw 2-2 with The Bairns to extend their unbeaten league record to 21 games. Gary Irvine, playing in midfield, scores his first goal for the club before Craig Forsyth draws level, scoring his third goal in three games, which is celebrated ecstatically by both players and fans.

## SATURDAY 20th MARCH 1999

Hearts visit Dens without a win since early December and with Steven Boyack making his debut after his £25,000 move from Rangers, an Eddie Annand double gives Dundee a 2-0 win. It is Dundee's fourth win over the season over the Jambos with the Dark Blues spurred on by being called a 'pub team' by Hearts players when they bumped into each other on holiday the previous summer.

## SATURDAY 21st MARCH 1896

Dundee Football Club hosts its first ever international match when Scotland face Wales in a British International Championship match. The Dark Blues' Bill Thomson and Sandy Keillor are in the side and Keillor becomes the first Dee to score for Scotland when he gets the second in a 4-0 win.

## SATURDAY 21st MARCH 1970

A week after losing 2-1 to Celtic at Hampden in the Scottish Cup semi-final, goals from Gordon Wallace and Jocky Scott earn Dundee a 2-1 win over Rangers in front of 15,000 at Dens.

## WEDNESDAY 21st MARCH 1973

Dundee's deadly front three all score to defeat Arbroath 6-0 at Dens in the top flight. Jocky Scott scores a hat-trick while John Duncan (2) and Gordon Wallace are also on the scoresheet. The trio would score 69 goals throughout the campaign.

## SATURDAY 22nd MARCH 1947

Dundee win 10-0 for the second game in a row to equal a club record, this time against Dunfermline Athletic at Dens. Albert Juliussen scores seven to set a club record of most goals in a game (shared now with Alan Gilzean's seven against Queen of the South in 1962) with Peter Rattray and Ernie Ewen (2) also on target. Dundee charge towards the Scottish League B Division title, scoring 15 goals in the remaining three games.

## WEDNESDAY 23rd MARCH 1910

Dundee beat Hibernian at the third time of asking in a 1-0 Scottish Cup semi-final win at Celtic Park. After two 0-0 draws at Easter Road and Dens, John 'Sailor' Hunter is the hero as his goal propels Dundee into their first Scottish Cup final.

## MONDAY 23rd MARCH 1960

Dundee hansel their new floodlights when they beat English Second Division side Liverpool 1-0 thanks to a Hugh Robertson goal. The Anfield club are managed by Bill Shankly, brother of Dundee boss Bob, with former Dark Blues goalkeeper Reuben Bennett – formerly Bob's assistant at Third Lanark – as coach. The coincidence of personalities goes even further, for on the very day Bob Shankly is appointed Dundee manager, the Dens directors received a late application from Huddersfield Town boss Bill Shankly.

## SATURDAY 23rd MARCH 1985

Stewart Rafferty, Robert Connor and Ray Stephen score to give Dundee a 3-1 win over Rangers in front of just 9,544 at Ibrox. It is Dundee's seventh win over Rangers since promotion in 1981.

## TUESDAY 24th MARCH 1925

After a 1-1 draw in front of 21,814 at Dens, Dundee defeat Hamilton Academical 2-0 at Easter Road in a Scottish Cup semi-final replay. Davie McLean and John Rankine's goals send Dundee to their second Scottish Cup final.

## SATURDAY 24th MARCH 1962

Bobby Waddell comes in to replace the injured Alan Gilzean and scores a priceless winner in a 1-0 victory over Hibernian at Dens. On a wet and windy afternoon, Waddell chases a long ball from Bobby Seith to shoot past Simpson from ten yards and Dundee's title chances are given a further boost when Rangers surprisingly lose 1-0 at Ibrox to Dundee United, allowing Dundee to pull within one point of the league leaders.

## SATURDAY 24th MARCH 1990

Keith Wright, Rab Shannon and a hurricane help Dundee beat Dundee United 2-1 at Tannadice. Paddy Connolly puts United ahead early on but suddenly a squall whips up as United keeper Alan Main tries to take a goal kick. With the ball struggling to reach the half way line, Maurice Malpas slices the ball into the air and hurls it back towards the United box. Keith Wright is on his toes and nips ahead of Main to head the ball into the empty net, with BBC commentator Archie Macpherson stating on *Sportscene* at night, 'goal scored by hurricane.' In truth it had been scored by 'The Mongoose' before Rab Shannon curls in a free kick to give Dundee a priceless 2-1 win and remain undefeated to The Arabs that season, taking six points from eight.

### SATURDAY 25th MARCH 1961

Dundee defeat Ayr United 6-1 at Dens thanks to goals from Hugh Robertson (2), Ronnie Crichton, Alan Gilzean (2) and Alan Cousin. Gilzean would finish top goalscorer with 32 goals in all competitions.

### SATURDAY 26th MARCH 2011

Dundee set a new club record of 23 league games unbeaten with a 2-2 draw at home to Cowdenbeath thanks to a double from Jake Hyde. Hyde plays his second and final game as a trialist for Dundee as March 31st is the last date the SFL allow players to be registered. The match against the Central Park side is a real six-pointer with the Blue Brazil now occupying the play-off spot. Hyde retains his place in the side after scoring against Dunfermline midweek and again getting permission from his junior club Lochee United to play. Dundee's astonishing unbeaten run starts after a defeat at Cowdenbeath and six months and a day later, it could have ended against the same side as Dundee have to come back twice from behind to grab a vital point.

### WEDNESDAY 27th MARCH 1968

After getting a third-round bye Dundee meet FC Zurich in the Inter-Cities Fairs Cup quarter-final. Earlier the Swiss side had beaten Barcelona, Nottingham Forest and Sporting Lisbon and on a windy night in front of 13,500 at Dens, a late scrambled goal by Jim Easton gives Dundee a 1-0 first leg win.

## SATURDAY 28th MARCH 1964

Dundee met Kilmarnock at Ibrox in the Scottish Cup semi-final. There is little between the sides as play rages from end to end and Dundee keeper Bert Slater makes a miraculous save from a point blank McIlroy header before Alan Gilzean breaks the deadlock from close range on the half hour. Andy Penman scores a second 17 minutes after the break and an own goal by Jim McFadzean in 77 minutes and another by Gilzean two minutes later gives Dundee a convincing 4-0 win and sends the Dark Blues into their fourth Scottish Cup final.

## SATURDAY 29th MARCH 1952

Billy Steel opts out of the Scotland v England international in an effort to be fit for Dundee's Scottish Cup semi-final meeting with Third Lanark at Easter Road. With his leg heavily strapped, Steel sets up Gerry Burrell with a brilliant dummy to open the scoring on 27 minutes before adding a second himself just before half time to send Dundee to their second major final of the season with a 2-0 win.

## SATURDAY 29th MARCH 2002

Lee Wilkie becomes the first Dundee player to score for Scotland in 38 years with the winner in a 2-1 European Championship qualifying win against Iceland at Hampden. In total, Wilkie would make 11 appearances for his country, making him the fourth most capped Scotland player in Dundee's history as well as winning a B cap and eight Under-21 caps.

## SATURDAY 30th MARCH 1974

Dundee defeat Dunfermline Athletic 5-1 in Fife thanks to a penalty from Jocky Scott and goals from Bobby Ford, Jimmy Wilson, Alex Pringle and Gordon Wallace. Scott would finish the season as top goalscorer with 29 goals.

## SATURDAY 31st MARCH 1894

Towards the end of Dundee's inaugural season, three Dundee players are called up for a British International Championship match against Ireland in Belfast to become Dundee's first internationalists. Goalkeeper Francis Barrett, captain William Longair and winger Sandy Keillor make history by playing in the 2-1 win at Cliftonville's ground, Solitude.

## SATURDAY 31st MARCH 1962

Manager Bob Shankly celebrates his daughter's engagement to Dundee United's Jimmy Briggs by capturing top spot as Rangers were on Scottish Cup semi-final duty. Twice Dundee are pegged back by Stirling Albion before half time when the side at the bottom equalise goals from Alan Cousin and Gordon Smith. Alan Gilzean marks his return from injury with the winning header 22 minutes from time from a Hugh Robertson corner.

# DUNDEE FC
# *On This Day*

# APRIL

## SATURDAY 1st APRIL 2006

Second Division Gretna were favourites against First Division Dundee in the Scottish Cup semi-final at Hampden and live up to their tag with a 3-0 win. Gretna take the lead right on half time when Kenny Deuchar capitalises on a defensive mistake and Ryan McGuffie makes it two just before the hour with a controversial penalty. Dundee's misery is complete when a Jamie McQuilken cross deflects off Barry Smith for the third. It's a result that is the final nail in manager Alan Kernaghan's coffin as he is sacked shortly afterwards.

## WEDNESDAY 2nd APRIL 1975

Dundee are paired with Celtic in the Scottish Cup semi-final at Hampden and Ronnie Glavin scores the only goal in a tight affair. He robs Dundee skipper Tommy Gemmell to send a low shot past Scotland international goalkeeper Thomson Allan from 12 yards.

## WEDNESDAY 3rd APRIL 1968

With a slender 1-0 first leg lead, Dundee come under intense pressure against FC Zurich in the Letzgrund Stadium in the Inter-Cities Fairs Cup quarter-final. Dundee leave George McLean up front on his own but ten minutes from half-time Sammy Wilson out jumps the home keeper to head a fine goal and send The Dee into the last four with a 2-0 aggregate win.

## WEDNESDAY 3rd APRIL 1974

Dundee draw Celtic in the Scottish Cup semi-final, aiming to reach both major finals of the season. However, Celtic get revenge for their League Cup final defeat in December when Jimmy Johnstone caps a dazzling display with the only goal at Hampden.

## SATURDAY 4th APRIL 1896

With the league season finishing in February, Dundee embarked on an April tour of England. On Easter Saturday a new British record crowd of 60,000 watches Corinthians defeat Dundee 3-1 at the Queen's Club, West Kensington in London (the venue of Queens Club Lawn Tennis Championship). Corinthians have four England internationals in their side but Dundee aren't helped when their goalkeeper Bill Coventry flogs two goals early in the match. By contrast, Corinthians keeper A.G.S. Lawrence from Cambridge University is in excellent form, repeatedly saving efforts from Dundee's Bill Thomson, Sandy Keillor, Bill Longair and Johnny Darroch. Keillor does manage to pull a goal back for the 'Ten Bobbers' but not before Corinthians have scored a third to win the match 3-1.

## MONDAY 4th APRIL 1949

Clyde exact revenge for their 1910 Scottish Cup final defeat by knocking Dundee out in the semi-final. After coming back from 2-0 to draw 2-2 at Easter Road nine days before, Dundee go ahead in the Hampden replay through an early Milligan own goal. However, a double from Bootland sends the Bully Wee through to the final.

## SATURDAY 5th APRIL 1930

Andy Campbell scores a hat-trick as Dundee defeat Ayr United 3-0 at Dens and would finish the season as top scorer with 20 goals. He would finish top marksman on four occasions and score 107 goals in 199 appearances.

## SATURDAY 6th APRIL 1918

Dundee win the Scottish League Eastern Division with a 2-0 victory over Cowdenbeath at Dens. Cowdenbeath go into the match knowing that a draw will be enough to win the league but a double from Tommy Taylor, who finishes the season as top scorer with 28 goals, is enough to give The Dee the wartime title, deemed official by the Scottish League.

## WEDNESDAY 6th APRIL 1977

For the fifth time since 1970, the Scottish Cup semi-final draw pairs Dundee with Celtic and the First Division Dee put up a good show in an enthralling encounter. However, two goals by Joe Craig in the last ten minutes sends Celtic through to the final.

## SATURDAY 7th APRIL 1894

Dundee defeat Newcastle United 8-2 in front of 5,000 at Carolina Port. With Dundee's inaugural league season finishing in March, a number of friendlies are arranged to complete their debut year and goals from Bill Thomson, Jimmy Dundas (3), Davie McInroy, Bill Longair (2) and Sandy Gilligan give Dundee a convincing win before a 2-1 defeat to Newcastle's north-east rivals Sunderland two days later.

## SATURDAY 7th APRIL 1962

An Andy Penman brace pushes Dundee closer to the Scottish title with a 2-1 win against Airdrieonians at Broomfield. The winner comes from the spot as 'Penalty King' Penman keeps his 100% record from 12 yards after Shanks fists the ball over the bar. Referee Willie Brittle misses the offence and the kick is only awarded after the Dundee players persuade the referee to consult his linesman.

## SATURDAY 7th APRIL 2001

Dundee go into the last match before the first ever SPL split at Aberdeen three points behind Dunfermline in sixth but with a superior goal difference. Without the injured Claudio Caniggia, Dundee had to wait until six minutes into the second half for Giorgi Nemsadze to give them the lead. Shortly afterwards, Fabian Caballero, in his first start since he ruptured a knee ligament against Dundee United in September, made it 2-0 to secure the Dark Blues' fifth successive win at Pittodrie. At full time there is still four minutes to play in Dunfermline's match at Rugby Park but when it is confirmed that Kilmarnock have won 2-1, there are wild celebrations amongst both players and fans as Dundee secure a top six spot.

## WEDNESDAY 8th APRIL 2015

Dundee recorded their first victory over Dundee United in ten years with a 3-1 win at Dens. Dundee opened the scoring when United goalkeeper Radoslaw Cierzniak allowed Greg Stewart's shot to squirm through his legs and into the net and the goal is voted Dundee's Goal of the Season at the end of season Player of Year Dinner. Nadir Ciftci equalised for The Arabs from the spot after Chris Erskine's effort strikes Kevin Thomson's arm but Stewart twice delivers perfectly for James McPake and Paul Heffernan to net, putting Dundee back in the top six and sparking wild celebrations in the home stands.

## SATURDAY 9th APRIL 1910

Dundee and Clyde meet in the Scottish Cup final at Ibrox. The Bully Wee start confidently and are 2-0 ahead at half time thanks to goals from Chalmers and Booth, both the result of poor Dundee defending. As the minutes tick away the Clyde ribbons are placed on the trophy but with three and a half minutes left, John 'Sailor' Hunter chases a long ball through the middle and when Clyde keeper Watson attempts to clear the ball, it flies off the inrushing forward and into the net. Then, with 30 seconds remaining, Dundee win a corner and when Jimmy Bellamy sends over the perfect cross, George Langlands crashes the ball into the net to make it 2-2 and send the final to a replay.

## MONDAY 9th APRIL 1956

Dundee defeat recently crowned English Champions Manchester United 5-1 at Dens. Bobby Charlton makes his debut for the Busby Babes but goals from George Merchant (3), Alan Cousin (his first for The Dee) and George O'Hara give the Dark Blues a famous friendly win against a side featuring three players who would later perish in the Munich air disaster in 1958.

## MONDAY 9th APRIL 1962

Easter Monday sees a rearranged Dundee derby originally postponed on January 2nd. A capacity Tannadice crowd witnesses Jim Irvine put Dundee United in front with a header after quarter of an hour before Alan Gilzean equalises a minute before half time. Then, with four minutes remaining, Gilzean scores the winner with a 25-yard thunderbolt which bounces over Ugolini in the United goal. It is a significant day in the title race as The Dee pull level with Rangers after they can only draw 1-1 with Celtic in the Old Firm derby.

## WEDNESDAY 9th APRIL 2003

After a 1-1 Scottish Cup quarter-final draw with Falkirk at the soon to be demolished Brockville, the sides meet again in the replay at Dens with Inverness Caledonian Thistle awaiting the winners. The Bairns dominate most of the first half and open the scoring on 31 minutes when Taylor thumps in an effort from outside the box. Fabian Caballero equalises two minutes from the break with a splendidly low shot, but with no further scoring the game goes into extra time. The introduction of two new strikers gives Dundee fresh impetus and the on-loan Mark Burchill scores to give the home side the lead for the first time in the tie. Steve Lovell nets a brace to seal a 4-1 win and send The Dee to Hampden.

## MONDAY 10th APRIL 1911

An R.C. Hamilton goal gives Dundee a 1-0 victory over Airdrieonians in front of 7,000 at Dens. The Scotland international would finish the season as top scorer with 20 goals as the Dark Blues finished sixth three games later.

## SATURDAY 11th APRIL 1925

Dundee lose the Scottish Cup Final 2-1 to Celtic in front of 75,137 at Hampden. Davie McLean gives the Dark Blues the lead on 30 minutes when he rushes in to net the rebound after Jock Gilmore's header hits the bar. Dundee sit back and defend in the second half and pay the price when Patsy Gallagher wriggles past several lunging tackles, traps the ball between his legs and somersaults into the net. With three minutes left, Jimmy McGrory heads home a MacFarlane free kick to give The Bhoys a 2-1 win and take the cup home to Celtic Park.

## SATURDAY 11th APRIL 1964

In front of 133,245 at Hampden, Dundee centre-forward Alan Gilzean scores the winner for Scotland in a British International Championship win over England. With just 12 minutes left, Gillie heads home a Davie Wilson corner past Gordon Banks to secure a 1-0 win and a hat-trick of wins over the 'Auld Enemy' for the only time in the 20th century.

## WEDNESDAY 11th APRIL 1973

Four days after drawing 0-0 with Celtic in the Scottish Cup semi-final, the sides are still goalless after another 90 minutes in the replay at the National Stadium. In extra time Jock Stein switches George Connelly to midfield and the move pays dividends as goals from Jimmy Johnstone (2) and Kenny Dalglish propel the Parkhead side into the final.

## SATURDAY 11th APRIL 1987

Despite appeals from both clubs to play the Scottish Cup semi-final in the City of Discovery, the SFA insist that Dundee and Dundee United meet at Tynecastle. Iain Ferguson gives United the lead just after the half hour but the Dark Blues fight back to lead at the break with goals from Tommy Coyne and Keith Wright. Ferguson levels on 54 minutes before Paul Hegarty puts The Arabs in front ten minutes later. Despite Dundee's pressure, they can't take the tie to a replay when Billy Thomson brilliantly saves twice from two John Brown free kicks.

### SATURDAY 11th APRIL 1998

Dundee win the Scottish League First Division title and promotion to the top flight after a 1-1 draw at Raith. Future Dundee manager Paul Hartley gives Rovers the lead shortly after half time before Eddie Annand heads Dundee into the inaugural SPL on the hour with four games of the campaign still to go.

### SUNDAY 12th APRIL 1970

Dundee finish the season with a 3-1 win over Heart of Midlothian at Tynecastle thanks to goals from Gordon Wallace (2) and Jocky Scott. The Dee finish in sixth place, two points behind the Jam Tarts and Dundee United.

### SATURDAY 13th APRIL 1901

Dundee win the Dewar Shield with a 6-1 win over East Stirlingshire at Dens. The Dewar Shield is competed for by the winners of the Aberdeenshire, Forfarshire, Perthshire and Stirlingshire Cup winners and goals from Fred McDiarmid, John Halkett (2), Tommy McDermott, David Steven and Archie McGeoch give The Dee their first win in the tournament.

### SATURDAY 14th APRIL 1984

Dundee meet holders Aberdeen in the Scottish Cup semi-final at Tynecastle and The Dons take the lead in 28 minutes when Ian Porteous scores from a cleverly worked corner. Dundee have the ball in the net three times but all efforts are disallowed by referee Brian McGinlay and in the final minute Gordon Strachan comes back to haunt his old club and settles matters with a second goal.

## SATURDAY 14th APRIL 1990

After a nine-year stay in the top flight, Dundee are relegated from the Premier Division after a 2-1 defeat at home to nearest rivals St Mirren. Alan Campbell gives Dundee the perfect start after just 65 seconds and they have a great chance to make it 2-0 when Keith Wright is brought down in the box. Billy Dodds smashes his penalty off the post and The Saints score two second half goals to send The Dee down.

## MONDAY 15th APRIL 1968

George McLean scores the 34th goal of his debut Dark Blue season as Dundee defeat Hearts 1-0 over in front of 8,000 at Dens. He would score his 35th and final goal of the campaign five days later in a 2-0 win at Raith.

## SATURDAY 16th APRIL 1960

Goals from Alan Gilzean and Hugh Robertson give Dundee a 2-0 win over Celtic in front of 16,000 at Dens as The Dee chase down a fourth-placed finish. The Dark Blues complete a league double over The Hoops after a 3-2 win at Celtic Park the previous December.

## SATURDAY 17th APRIL 1965

Dundee defeat Third Lanark 6-1 in the penultimate league game of the season at Dens. Goals from Jocky Scott (2), Andy Penman (2), Alan Cousin and Charlie Cooke help secure a sixth-placed finish for the second year in a row.

## SATURDAY 18th APRIL 1998

Dundee received the Scottish League First Division trophy after a 1-1 draw with Ayr United in front of 8,104 fans at Dens, their largest home league gate of the season. James Grady scores the equaliser from the spot but later misses another penalty before captain Barry Smith picks up the trophy in the centre circle at full time.

## SUNDAY 18th APRIL 1999

With construction of the new stands behind the goals underway to meet the SPL ground criteria, Dundee's home match with Rangers is moved to Tannadice. Having lost 4-0 and 6-1 to Rangers earlier in the season, manager Jocky Scott changes his formation to a 4-3-3 with Iain Anderson in a wide-left attacking goal. Anderson is at his tantalising best and heads home a Steven Boyack cross on 22 minutes before Tony Vidmar levels just after the break. Post-match Rangers manager Dick Advocaat tells the press, 'On that form Dundee would have taken points from any team on the planet."

### TUESDAY 18th APRIL 2000

Against bottom placed Aberdeen, Paco Luna is the target for some tough tackling Dons at Pittodrie. After being booked the Spaniard is substituted for fear of a red card for retaliating and his replacement, countryman Javier Artero, sees skill win the day when he scores a last minute winner with a finely struck shot from the edge of the box.

### SATURDAY 19th APRIL 1952

Dundee lose 4-0 to Motherwell in the Scottish Cup final in front of 136,990 at Hampden; a Scottish club record attendance for a match not involving either of the Old Firm. At half-time the scoreline is blank and Dundee are unlucky not to be ahead after Well skipper Willie Kilmarnock kicks the ball off the line three times. Motherwell grow in confidence and score two goals within a minute just after the break and another lightning double near the end sends the cup to Lanarkshire.

### SATURDAY 19th APRIL 1980

Dundee gave themselves a chance of staying up when they stun league leaders Celtic with a 5-1 win at Dens. Roy Aitken gives The Bhoys a five-minute lead but in a remarkable turnaround two goals by 17-year-old Iain Ferguson and one from Ian Fleming before the break and then Eric Sinclair and Peter Mackie in the second half, earns the Dark Blues a famous victory. It is capped off by Ally Donaldson saving a Murdo MacLeod penalty after Jim Shirra punches the ball over the bar, earning himself a booking. However, within the next four days both Kilmarnock and Partick Thistle win their games in hand to relegate Dundee in ninth place in front of bottom club Hibs.

## WEDNESDAY 20th APRIL 1910

Dundee win the Scottish Cup with a 2-1 second replay victory over Clyde at Ibrox. The Dee are shocked when Chalmers puts the Shawfielders ahead after three minutes but Jimmy Bellamy heads the equaliser from a 15th minute corner. Ten minutes after the break, John 'Sailor' Hunter writes his name into Dark Blue folklore when he breaks through on goal and, after beating former Dens Park centre-half McAteer, sends the ball past McTurk to win the cup for Dundee. Hunter is inducted into the club's Hall of Fame with a Heritage Award in 2016.

## SUNDAY 20th APRIL 2003

Georgi Nemsadze scores the winner as Dundee defeat Inverness Caledonian Thistle 1-0 in the Scottish Cup semi-final at Hampden. Rangers have already qualified for the Champions League and are awaiting the victors in the final. The win not only sends The Dee into their first Scottish Cup final since 1964 but also into premier European competition for the first time in 29 years. Nemsadze is inducted into the Dundee FC Hall of Fame in 2010 with an International Award.

## WEDNESDAY 21st APRIL 1976

A crowd of 13,800 descend upon Dens to witness a Tommy Gemmell penalty and an Eric Sinclair goal give Dundee a 2-1 win over Dundee United at Dens. It is the Dark Blues' second 2-1 win over The Arabs that season.

## TUESDAY 22nd APRIL 1969

Dundee defeat Rangers 3-2 at Dens in the first of a double header with the Light Blues. Goals from Alex Bryce (2) and Joe Gilroy secure the win before a 1-1 draw at Ibrox six days later.

## SATURDAY 23rd APRIL 1947

Dundee clinch the Scottish League B Division title with a 5-2 win in front of 10,000 fans at Dens Park. The goals come from Ernie Ewen, Albert Juliussen (3) and Johnny Pattillo and this time Dundee are granted promotion to the top flight after having been denied the year before. Despite winning the second tier, the previous season is

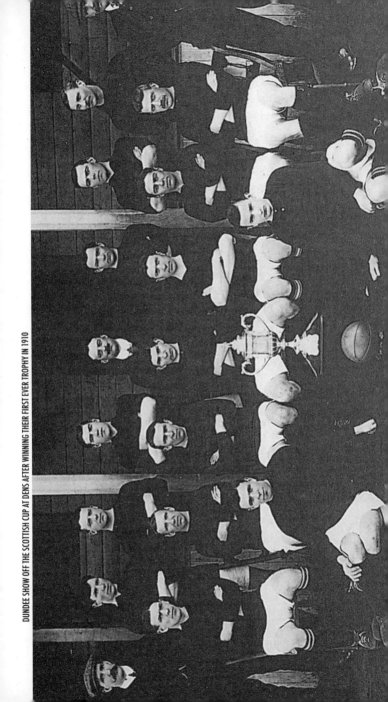

DUNDEE SHOW OFF THE SCOTTISH CUP AT DENS AFTER WINNING THEIR FIRST EVER TROPHY IN 1910

deemed unofficial by the Scottish League. The Dee would finish the season the following week with a 6-2 home win over Ayr and their goal tally for the season amounts to an impressive 134 goals in 35 league and cup games.

### SATURDAY 23rd APRIL 1994

A 2-0 home defeat to Celtic finally confirms Dundee's relegation from the top flight which had been on the cards for weeks. The Dark Blues finish bottom of a 12-team Premier Division, 11 points from safety, and winning just 8 games out of 44.

### SATURDAY 23rd APRIL 2011

Dundee overturn the 25-point penalty to secure survival with a 1-0 win at Ross County. In many ways it is a performance which sums up much of the post-administration season as they defend superbly when under pressure, ride their luck when former Dee Stevie Milne hits the underside of the bar, playing some neat passing football, grinding out a result when most needed and seeing a youngster come to the fore by grabbing the winning goal. That goal comes from Leighton McIntosh in 65 minutes when he takes advantage of a poor touch from Michael McGovern to take the ball off the County keeper before rolling it into the empty net in front of a jubilant 608 away fans. While the day before had been Good Friday, it turns out to be a good Saturday for The Dee as the final whistle brings scenes of joy. Players, management and fans celebrate the amazing feat of what they have achieved in staying up after the 25-point deduction from the Scottish League with two games to spare and it will be an achievement long remembered.

### WEDNESDAY 24th APRIL 1963

Dundee travel to Italy to face AC Milan in the European Cup semi-final first leg and the kick off is delayed 13 minutes to allow in the large 78,000 crowd. Sani gives the Rossoneri the lead when he heads home after just three minutes but midway through the half, Alan Cousin becomes the first British player to score in the San Siro when he heads an Andy Penman cross into the net. In the second half Milan score another four goals from crosses when they repeatedly put high balls on top of Alex Hamilton and every time goalkeeper

Bert Slater goes up to catch the ball, he is blinded by a battery of cameramen firing flashbulbs around the goal. Milan win 5-1 but referee Caballero is later banned for life for receiving bribes from the Italians.

## WEDNESDAY 25th APRIL 1962

Dundee host St Mirren in the penultimate match of the 1961/62 season. Joint top of the league with Rangers, Alan Cousin puts Dundee ahead shortly before half-time with a low shot from 18 yards but with 12 minutes remaining The Saints are awarded a penalty when Gordon Smith is adjudged to have handled. Remembering advice from his St Mirren-supporting father, Paisley-born goalkeeper Pat Liney dives towards the top left hand corner to claw away Jim Clunie's penalty and four minutes later Andy Penman makes it 2-0. Jubilant fans invade the pitch when they learn Rangers have lost 1-0 at Pittodrie meaning The Dee are top and now need only a point to become champions of Scotland. Pat Liney's place in Dark Blue history is assured and he is inducted into the club's Hall of Fame in 2011 with a Legends Award. He is appointed Honorary President later the same year.

## SATURDAY 25th APRIL 1964

Dundee lose 3-1 to Rangers in the Scottish Cup final in front of 120,982 at Hampden. Willie Henderson heads Rangers into the lead on 71 minutes but 60 seconds later Kenny Cameron scores one of the greatest goals ever seen at the National Stadium when he turns and hooks a superb volley home from a long ball into the box from the restart from Alex Stuart. Dundee's goalkeeper makes a series of superb saves and the final would become known as the 'Bert Slater Final'. However, two late goals from Jimmy Millar and Ralph Brand in the final minute sends the cup to Govan.

## SATURDAY 25th APRIL 1992

Dundee win promotion to the Premier Division with a 3-1 home win over Forfar Athletic at Dens. Goals from John McQuillan, Paul Ritchie (thrust into the side after scoring four against Forfar's reserves earlier in the week) and Eddie Gallagher guarantees a return to the top flight after a two-year gap.

## SATURDAY 26th APRIL 1952

Dundee finished their successful League Cup-winning season with a 6-0 home win over Third Lanark. The goals come from George Christie, a hat-trick by Bobby Flavell and a double by Albert Henderson. At the end of the match there is a special cheer for Johnny Pattillo who has played his last game for Dundee before taking up his coaching post at Pittodrie and he is carried off shoulder high by teammates Doug Cowie and Alfie Boyd. After six successful years at Dens, he had scored 67 goals in 172 appearances and heads back to the Granite City with a B Division winners' medal and a Scottish League Cup winners' medal in his pocket. Johnny gets both his medals after the win over Third Lanark when the players and officials are invited into the Dens Park boardroom by chairman James Gellatly to be presented with their League Cup winners' medals. The Scottish League didn't present winners' medals until 1957 and so Dundee are granted permission to issue their own to players and backroom staff. The players who were part of the 1946/47 B Division championship team five years earlier are also presented with winners' medals and Mr Gellatly explains that it has taken so long to present them because there has been a difficulty getting the gold for them.

## SATURDAY 26th APRIL 2014

Dundee win 3-0 away at Alloa Athletic on a crucial day in the SPFL Championship winning season. Having lost in Greenock the previous week, goals from Christian Nade, Peter MacDonald and Craig Beattie see the title swing back in Dundee's favour as rivals Hamilton Academical surprisingly lose 4-1 at Dumbarton.

## SATURDAY 27th APRIL 1946

Albert Juliussen scores twice as Dundee defeat Hibernian 2-0 in front of 20,000 at Dens in the first round, second leg of the Scottish Victory Cup. Hibs, however, progress 3-2 on aggregate after winning 3-0 at Easter Road the week before.

## SATURDAY 28th APRIL 1962

The greatest day in the history of Dundee Football Club as they win the Scottish League Division One title with a 3-0 victory over St

Johnstone at Muirton Park, Perth. In front of 26,500, Saints need a point to stay up while Dundee need a point for the title and both teams are affected by the tension early on. On 24 minutes Alan Gilzean sends the large travelling support wild when he heads in Gordon Smith's swirling cross from the right. Dundee then control the game and on the hour Gilzean runs on to a brilliant long ball from Alex Hamilton and beats centre-half Jim Ferguson before cracking home his 27th goal of the season. Eight minutes later Andy Penman crashes in a third via the crossbar from the edge of the box, and with Rangers drawing 1-1 with Kilmarnock, Dundee win the League Flag by three points. The Saints are relegated on goal average behind Airdrie and St Mirren and chaos reigns at full time as thousands invade the pitch to acclaim the champions of Scotland. The team then travel back to Dundee to meet their jubilant fans in the city square and it is a fitting climax to a wonderful season.

## SATURDAY 29th APRIL 1939

Dundee and Montrose end their league campaign with a remarkable 5-5 draw at Links Park in the Dark Blues' highest ever scoring drawn match. Dundee's goals are scored by George Stewart, Johnstone Melville (2), Archie Coats and Charlie McGillivray, who finishes the season as top scorer with 29 goals.

## TUESDAY 29th APRIL 1986

Midfielder Robert Connor becomes Dundee's only internationalist of the eighties when he makes his Scotland debut in a friendly against the Netherlands in Eindhoven. Aberdeen manager Alex Ferguson was in charge for 0-0 draw and although he doesn't take Connor to Mexico for the World Cup in the summer, he signs him for The Dons in August for a fee of £275,000 plus Ian Angus.

## SATURDAY 30th APRIL 1938

Dundee are relegated for their first time in their history after drawing with Ayr United at Dens. A win would guarantee survival but with virtually the same team which had won 5-1 at Somerset Park just three weeks before, they can only manage a 0-0 draw to finish 19th in a 20 team league, one point behind six teams, including Ayr.

## SATURDAY 30th APRIL 2011

Dundee beat Partick Thistle 3-2 at Dens before celebrating the achievement of overcoming the 25-point penalty. Almost 8,000 fans turn up on a beautiful sunny afternoon to cheer their Dundee heroes and, after watching a goalless first half, enjoy a Craig Forsyth double and a Matt Lockwood penalty after the break to ensure Dundee are now 15 months unbeaten at home as well as having suffered just one loss in the last 28 league games. The final whistle sees the players head back up the tunnel before being introduced back on to the pitch one by one to a huge cheer and a standing ovation. Each of the squad wears a white t-shirt with the message '-25 Mission Impossible...' on the front and 'Thanks to all our Dee-Fiant fans' on the back and after manager Barry Smith comes out to a rapturous reception, they all go on a pre-arranged lap of honour around all four sides of the ground. Both players and fans acknowledge each others' remarkable efforts during the season with plenty of cheering, clapping and scarf-waving.

# DUNDEE FC
# *On This Day*

# MAY

## WEDNESDAY 1st MAY 1963

Encouraged by the roars from a vociferous 38,000 crowd, Dundee defeat AC Milan 1-0 in the European Cup semi-final second leg. Alan Gilzean scores the winner when he rises to head a Gordon Smith cross past Italian goalkeeper Ghezzi but is later sent off with six minutes remaining for lashing out at Peruvian marker Benitez who had dished out some terrible punishment to Gillie in both legs. Milan progress to Wembley 5-2 on aggregate but the Dark Blues have done Scotland proud, coming so close to being the first British side to reach the European Cup final.

## WEDNESDAY 1st MAY 1968

Dundee draw 1-1 with Leeds United in the Inter-Cities Fairs Cup semi-final first leg in front of 24,000 at Dens. Paul Madeley heads past Ally Donaldson to give Leeds a 26th minute lead but Bobby Wilson draws Dundee level ten minutes later with an opportunistic header after Alex Kinninmonth's header is cleared off the line by Terry Cooper.

## THURSDAY 1st MAY 1976

Dundee beat Motherwell 1-0 at Dens in their final game of the inaugural Premier Division thanks to an Eric Sinclair winner. After news comes through at full time of Ayr United's 5-3 home defeat to Celtic, there are wild celebrations on the terracing on the assumption Dundee are safe from relegation. It isn't to be however as on May 3rd Ayr beat Motherwell 2-1 at home and two days later Dundee United battle to a shock 0-0 draw with league champions Rangers at Ibrox. This leaves Dundee one point behind Ayr and on the same points as Aberdeen and Dundee United, but an inferior goal difference sends The Dee down.

## SATURDAY 1st MAY 1999

Goals from Brian Irvine and James Grady give Dundee a famous 2-0 win over Dundee Utd at Tannadice, securing Dundee's first league finish ahead of United for 25 years. Irvine gives the dominant Dee the lead in 67 minutes when he heads home a Hugh Robertson corner and Grady rounds off a glorious day in the final minute by latching on to Steven Boyack's through ball and slipping it between Sieb Dykstra's legs.

DOON! DUNDEE FAN CRAIG WIGHTON ENJOYS HIS 93RD MINUTE WINNER WHICH IS THE FINAL NAIL IN DUNDEE UNITED'S RELEGATION COFFIN

## SATURDAY 2nd MAY 1981

Dundee secure promotion back to the Premier Division at the first attempt with a 1-0 win at East Stirlingshire on the final day of the season. Eric Sinclair is the hero when on 32 minutes Jimmy Murphy drifts a corner to the back post which Bobby Glennie nods back across and Sinky is on hand to head home and send Dundee up in second place behind champions Hibs.

## SATURDAY 2nd MAY 1992

Despite losing 2-1 at home to already relegated Montrose, Dundee win the Scottish League First Division title as Partick can only draw and are unable to overturn Dundee's pre-match two-point and seven-goal advantage. Captain Gordon Chisholm is presented with the trophy next to the tunnel after a pitch invasion stops the handover taking place in the centre circle.

## MONDAY 2nd MAY 2016

'The Doon Derby'. Dundee relegate their neighbours with a 2-1 win on a never-to-be-forgotten night at a raucous Dens Park. Edward Ofere gives Dundee United the lead on 54 minutes but with a draw good enough to send The Arabs down to the Championship, Kostadin Gadzhalov's 77th minute header effectively sends them 'doon'. Local boy and Dundee fan Craig Wighton then writes himself into Dark Blue folklore when he side-foots home from just inside the box three minutes into injury time to hit the final nail into United's coffin and send the home fans wild.

## SATURDAY 3rd MAY 1986

Hearts come to Dens on the final day of the season needing just a draw to become champions of Scotland while Dundee needed a win to maximise their European hopes. On an astonishing day in the history of Scottish football, the title looks to be heading to Gorgie with seven minutes left as the scoreline is blank, but rumours sweep Dens Park that Motherwell have gone ahead at Ibrox, meaning a win would send Dundee into the Uefa Cup. The Dee start to exert tremendous pressure and when Robert Connor sends in a wicked in-swinging corner, John Brown heads it on to substitute Albert Kidd to lash the ball past Henry Smith. Kidd had only started five games all season and four minutes later he picks the ball up in his own half, charges forward and plays a one-two with Graham Harvey before smashing in an incredible second. Dundee's 2-0 win, coupled with Celtic's 5-0 win at St Mirren, means the title goes to Parkhead on goal difference and with Rangers in fact winning 2-0 there is no Uefa Cup place for Dundee.

## SATURDAY 3rd MAY 2014

Dundee return to the top flight at the first time of asking when they win the SPFL Championship after a 2-1 win over Dumbarton at a sold out Dens Park. Goals from Christian Nade and top scorer Peter MacDonald set the Dark Blues on their way before an Agnew penalty for The Sons makes it a nervy last 20 minutes. News filters through that Hamilton are 10-2 up against Morton, which would be enough of a goal difference swing to give them the title in the event of a draw at Dens. It takes an incredible last minute save from Player of the Year Kyle Letheren to ensure captain Gavin Rae gets to lift the trophy on the pitch after it is delivered by helicopter at full time; the same trophy presented to Bobby Cox in 1962.

## SATURDAY 4th MAY 1957

League championship winner Hugh Robertson signs from junior side Auchinleck Talbot initially on a part-time contract. The former miner makes his debut in September that year, away at Aberdeen and the left-winger goes on to score 61 goals in 292 appearances over the next eight years. Shug would score six goals in 33 appearances in the 1962 title winning season and would play in five matches en route to the European Cup semi-finals the following year, scoring once in the 8-1 win over Cologne in the first round. Robertson is inducted into the club's Hall of Fame in 2012 with a Legends Award.

## WEDNESDAY 4th MAY 1983

Dundee defeat Rangers 2-1 at Dens thanks to goals from Iain Ferguson and Eric Sinclair to keep their Uefa Cup hopes alive in the penultimate home game of the season. It is Dundee's third consecutive home win over the Light Blues.

## SATURDAY 4th MAY 1985

In Dundee's last away game of the season, a John Brown goal gives Dundee a 1-0 win over Celtic in front of just 8,815 at Parkhead.

## SATURDAY 5th MAY 1956

Dundee defeat Dundee United 2-1 at Dens Park in the Forfarshire Cup semi-final thanks to goals from Jimmy Chalmers and Billy Birse, but more importantly Bobby Cox signs for Dundee from Junior side Dundee Osborne. Cox would captain Dundee to the 1962 Scottish League championship and would make 434 appearances; the second most in the club's history. Known as 'Sir Bobby' to the fans, Cox is inducted into the inaugural Dundee FC Hall of Fame in 2009 with a Legends Award to arguably the loudest cheer of the night. A Dundee supporter, born and bred in the city, for many Bobby Cox had simply lived our dream and we loved him for it.

## SUNDAY 5th MAY 2013

Having looked doomed for much of the season, Dundee make a good fist of staying up after John Brown is appointed manager in February but are relegated after failing to beat Aberdeen at Dens. The Dark Blues go ahead on 20 minutes after a superb volley from Jim McAllister into the top right-hand corner of the net. It looks like The Dee might take their fight to another week but with 20 minutes left, Peter Pawlett goes down easily in the box and Niall McGinn levels from the spot. The 1-1 draw consigns Dundee to the second tier after just one season in the top flight.

## SATURDAY 6th MAY 2000

Goals from Willie Falconer (2) and James Grady give Dundee a 3-0 win over Dundee United at Dens; their first home win over The Arabs in 11 years.

## SUNDAY 7th MAY 1967

Dundee defeat Buffalo 12-1 on the first game of their post-season tour of North America thanks to goals from Jocky Scott (3), Jim McLean (3), George McLean (2), Kenny Cameron, Alex Stuart, Steve Murray and Alex Hamilton.

## SATURDAY 8th MAY 1999

The Dark Blues overcome Aberdeen 2-1 at Pittodrie thanks to goals from Steven Boyack and Iain Anderson; their first league win over The Dons since Hogmanay 1988 and their first league success at

CAPTAIN GAVIN RAE CRADLES THE SCOTTISH CHAMPIONSHIP TROPHY AFTER WINNING THE TITLE ON A DRAMATIC FINAL DAY

Pittodrie since March 1976. The Dee would finish fifth two weeks later, equalling their highest finish since 1975.

## SATURDAY 9th MAY 1987

Dundee beat Hamilton Academical 7-3 in the last game of the season at Dens thanks to goals from John Brown, Keith Wright (3), Rab Shannon, Tommy Coyne and Graham Harvey. The seven goals gave The Dee 100 goals in all competitions across the season.

## SATURDAY 10th MAY 1958

Dundee end their season with a 1-0 win over runners-up Rangers at Ibrox thanks to an Alan Cousin goal. Pat Liney makes his debut in goal after World Cup bound Bill Brown was sent home with a virus and Cousin finishes the season as top scorer with 23 goals.

## THURSDAY 10th MAY 1979

Dundee win the Scottish League First Division title after a 2-2 draw with Ayr United in front of 7,692 at Dens. In the heavy rain, Ian Redford heads home an Erich Schaedler cross just before half time, only for McLaughlin and McSherry to put Ayr 2-1 ahead with 22 minutes left. On 77 minutes, Ian Redford heads his second to equalise and send Dundee back to the Premier Division at the third time of asking as champions.

## SATURDAY 11th MAY 1985

On a warm sunny day at Dens, 14,000 see Robert Connor score the only goal on the last day of the season to defeat Dundee United. Bobby Geddes saves his fifth penalty of the season (seven if you include two saves in reserve matches) from Tommy Coyne to secure the 1-0 win, the Dark Blues' first home derby win in six years.

## SATURDAY 12th MAY 1984

An Iain Ferguson double finishes the season with a 2-0 home win over St Johnstone as the Dark Blues confirm survival at the expense of the Saints. The Perth side had needed to win 9-0 to stay up due to the Dark Blues' vastly superior goal difference.

## SATURDAY 13th MAY 1995

Dundee defeat Stranraer 5-0 but miss out on the First Division title by a point and the play-offs on goal difference. On a bright, sunny day at Stair Park, Jim Hamilton gave Dundee the lead from the spot on nine minutes but don't get their second until Morten Weighorst scores on 62 minutes. Three goals in the last ten minutes from Weighorst, George Shaw and Paul Tosh are not enough for The Dee as they are two goals short of the play-off. There is some solace for the 1,200 Dees in attendance as Dundee United are relegated from the Premier Division at Tannadice, meaning a return for the derby next season.

## SATURDAY 13th MAY 2001

A Fabian Caballero double gives ten-man Dundee a 2-0 win over Celtic at Parkhead. Zurab Khizanishvili is sent off after a tussle with Henrik Larsson with Dundee already 1-0 up but a famous victory is secured against the already crowned SPL champions. It also gives The Dee victories over both halves of the Old Firm in Glasgow in the same season.

## TUESDAY 14th MAY 1968

Dundee lose their final game of the season 1-0 to Leeds United at Elland Road in the Inter-Cities Fairs Cup semi-final, second leg. Leeds had already knocked out Hibs and Rangers and progress to the final 2-1 on aggregate and would win the trophy with a 1-0 aggregate win over Ferencváros of Hungary.

## SATURDAY 15th MAY 2004

Dundee finished a traumatic administration season on a high when a last minute Steve Lovell goal gives Dundee a 2-1 win over Aberdeen at Pittodrie. Steven Milne had given Dundee the lead and the victory sees the Dark Blues finish top of the bottom six.

## SATURDAY 16th MAY 1953

Dundee's first match of their two month tour of South Africa takes place against Southern Transvaal in Johannesburg. When they take to the field in front of 22,000, they are wearing not their regular dark blue shirts but rather an Anderson tartan strip with a Dundee badge on the left breast, chosen by manager George Anderson. Bobby Flavell gets Dundee's strike in the 1-1 draw.

## THURSDAY 16th MAY 1963

An Alan Cousin goal gives Dundee a 1-0 win over Dunfermline Athletic in front of 12,000 at Dens in the penultimate home game of the European Cup season.

## SATURDAY 17th MAY 1947

A Dens Park crowd of 14,000 witnesses Dundee win the Forfarshire Cup with a 5-0 victory over Dundee United at Dens thanks to goals from Albert Juliussen (4) and Johnny Pattillo. The win comes just a month after winning the delayed 1945/46 Forfarshire Cup with a 6-1 victory over Forfar at Dens and a 6-5 semi-final win over Montrose at Links Park three days later.

## SATURDAY 18th MAY 1963

Alan Gilzean's 41st goal of the season helps Dundee defeat Falkirk 2-0 at Brockville in their last away game of the season. Thirty-nine year-old Gordon Smith scores the second in what is his last goal for the club.

## WEDNESDAY 19th MAY 1965

In the second year of the Summer Cup, Dundee beat St Johnstone 3-2 at Muirton in a Group One sectional tie thanks to a double from Kenny Cameron (2) and a Richmond own goal.

## SATURDAY 20th MAY 1893

Dundee Football Club are formed with the merger of Our Boys and East End at a meeting at Mathers Hotel in Whitehall Place where a formal application for membership of the Scottish League is prepared for submission to the Scottish Football League Annual General Meeting on June 12th.

## SUNDAY 20th MAY 1962

Dundee travel to America to take part in the prestigious annual New York Tourney. The tournament sees two groups of six compete against each other on Randall's Island and the Dark Blues' first match is against West German side Reutlingen. In front of a crowd of 17,500, on a pitch littered with nuts and bolts, Dundee lose 2-0 in tropical temperatures and humidity. The thermometer is now reading 99°F (37°F) and the Dundee coaching staff are constantly throwing bottles of water to the players. Alan Gilzean remembers that at half-time none of the exhausted players looked forward to going out for the second half and that Gordon Smith, (who would turn thirty-eight five days later), in particular was struggling. 'Gordon was knackered,' recalls Gillie, 'and said to us that he was going to pack it in after this and we had to persuade him that we were all just as knackered. Even at his age, Gordon was amongst the fittest players in the squad and we all struggled to cope with the heat and humidity in America.'

## SATURDAY 21st MAY 1955

Alan Cousin signed for Dundee from Alloa YMCA and remains part-time throughout his 11 years at Dens. A prolific centre-forward, scoring 141 times in 384 appearances, Cousin is part of the Dundee side to win the Scottish League title in 1962, reach the European Cup semi-final the year after and the Scottish Cup final the year after that. He is inducted into the club's Hall of Fame with a Legends Award in 2011.

## SUNDAY 21st MAY 1967

As part of Dundee's 11-game unbeaten tour of the USA, the Dark Blues defeat English champions Manchester United 4-2 in San Francisco thanks to goals from Sammy Wilson (2), Alex Bryce and Billy Campbell.

## SATURDAY 21st MAY 2005

Dundee go into the last game of the SPL season in bottom place but just two points behind Livingston whom they face at Almondvale. A win will guarantee Dundee safety and the gates in the 3,700 seat away section are closed at 2.45pm, forcing many more Dees to watch the win-or-bust tie from the hill outside. Dundee began well and in 17 minutes Bobby Mann heads back across goal from a corner and Callum Macdonald side-footed home. Livingston soon equalise when the controversial Hassan Kachloul crosses for Craig Easton to head in at the back post and the hosts then sit back and defend the draw which would keep them up. In the sixth minute of injury time Tam McManus hits a shot off the post but the game finishes 1-1 to send The Dee down. Dundee's points total of 38 is to date the highest ever won by a relegated side.

## SUNDAY 22nd MAY 1949

Dundee lose 2-1 to Beerschot Antwerp in the first game of their post-season seven-game tour of Belgium and Denmark. The Dee's consolation goal is scored by centre-forward Alec Stott.

## SATURDAY 23rd MAY 1953

Dundee defeat Natal 5-0 in Durban in the third game of the South African tour. The win is secured thanks to goals from Bobby Flavell (2), Billy Steel, Doug Cowie and an Alfie Boyd penalty.

## THURSDAY 24th MAY 1923

The summer of 1923 sees Dundee undertake their first overseas tour. A lengthy journey by boat and train takes them to Spain and two goals from Davie Halliday gives the Dark Blues a 2-0 win over Real Madrid in their new 22,500 capacity Estadio Charmartin. Dundee captain Jock Ross is presented to King Alfonso after the game.

## THURSDAY 25th MAY 1967

Dundee defeat FA Cup winners Chelsea 4-2 in Los Angeles thanks to goals from Jim McLean (2), George McLean and Sammy Wilson. It gives the Dark Blues 4-2 wins over both the English league champions and cup holders in their tour of the USA.

## SATURDAY 26th MAY 1923

A third tour brace from Davie Halliday and a goal from Willie Cowan gives Dundee a 3-0 win over Valencia. It is Dundee's fifth match of their Spanish tour after opening with a double header against Spanish champions Athletic Bilbao. Halliday scores his first brace in a 3-0 win in the opening match on May 20th which was followed up with a 1-1 draw the following day.

## SUNDAY 27th MAY 1923

Twenty-four hours later Dundee defeat Valencia again, this time 1-0 in front of 6,000 spectators and left-winger Jock McDonald, playing at inside-right, scores the winner. Before the match skipper Jock Ross is presented with a huge bouquet of flowers, mounted on a stick, which is so big he can hardly carry it.

## WEDNESDAY 27th MAY 1953

Dundee win 5-0 for the second game in a row of their South African tour against a Border XI in East London. Ronnie Turnbull scores twice alongside Bert Henderson and Billy Steel nets a penalty. Doug Cowie gets the fifth and has now scored the same number of goals on the tour as in his entire seven-year Dundee career to date.

## SUNDAY 28th MAY 1972

Dundee defeat New South Wales 6-1 in their tour of Australia and New Zealand thanks to goals from John Duncan (3), Dave Johnston, Bobby Wilson and Jocky Scott. The Dee would win all seven games of the tour, scoring 53 goals.

## THURSDAY 29th MAY 1986

Dundee defeat San Jose Earthquakes 4-0 on their tour of USA and Canada thanks to goals from Albert Kidd (2), Graham Harvey and Derek McWilliams.

## WEDNESDAY 30th MAY 1951

As part of the Festival of Britain clubs are encouraged to go on tour to promote the country and its national sport and Dundee go on a one-month tour of Israel and Turkey. They become the first side from the United Kingdom to tour Israel since it declared independence from the British Mandate for Palestine in 1948. That declaration had led to the Arab-Israeli conflict but since the 1949 Armistice Agreement, the region had been deemed more stable and the British government are delighted that Dundee were to 'fly the flag' in their former protectorate. A side touring from abroad is therefore a great novelty for the Israeli footballing fans and an impressive 50,000 turn up for the game in Tel Aviv in Dundee's first match against Maccabi. The game officially opens the new stadium but The Dee spoil the party with a 2-0 win thanks to goals from Bobby Flavell and Ernie Copland.

## SATURDAY 30th MAY 1953

Dundee's free-scoring form on their South African tour continues with a 5-0 win over Eastern Province in Port Elizabeth with goals from Dave Easson (2), Ronnie Turnbull and George Christie.

## WEDNESDAY 31st MAY 1961

Gordon Smith signs for Dundee at the age of 37 after being given a free transfer from Heart of Midlothian. He would become a key man in Dundee's side and, 11 months later, would pick up his third Scottish League winners' medal, making him the only man to win three championship medals with three different clubs (Hibs, Hearts and Dundee) outwith the Old Firm. He is inducted into Dundee's Hall of Fame in 2012 with a Legends Award with the award being accepted on stage at the Caird Hall by son Tony who has written his biography.

## TUESDAY 31st MAY 1986

Dundee face Manchester City in a challenge match in San Jose, USA and after a 1-1 draw in which Robert Connor scores for The Dee, the Sky Blues won on penalties.

## SATURDAY 31st MAY 2003

Dundee lose 1-0 to Rangers in the Scottish Cup final at Hampden Park but with Rangers winning the SPL and qualifying for the Champions League, Dundee's first Scottish Cup final appearance in 39 years sends them into the Uefa Cup. Almost 20,000 Dees travel to the National Stadium to watch their heroes and it might have been a glorious day had skipper Barry Smith's 25-yard shot in the fourth minute been six inches to the right and not struck the post.

# DUNDEE FC
## *On This Day*

# JUNE

## SUNDAY 1st JUNE 1924

After the success of their Spanish tour the summer before, Dundee return to Spain and in their first match defeat Barcelona 2-0. The heat was described by forward Davie McLean in a letter to The Courier as 'really awful' but in front of a 20,000 crowd, his strike partner Davie Halliday opened the scoring in 15 minutes after breaking through the Catalan defence. Halliday got a second after the break to secure the win and Dundee became the first side from outside Spain to have defeated both Real Madrid and Barcelona in their own stadiums.

## THURSDAY 2nd JUNE 1949

Dundee defeat a Copenhagen Select 4-2 in front of 20,000 on their tour of Belgium and Denmark thanks to goals from Jimmy Fraser (2), Tommy Gallacher and George Stewart.

## FRIDAY 2nd JUNE 1967

Dundee defeat Miami Cobras 3-1 with goals from Jocky Scott (2) and Jim McLean. The Dark Blues would be unbeaten in eleven games on their tour of North America with ten wins and one draw.

## SUNDAY 2nd JUNE 1985

Dundee are back in America for a tour of the US and Canada and in their first game a George McGeachie goal gives them a 1-0 win over FC Seattle in front of 4,487. The match was the first ever game the Dark Blues played on Astroturf.

## SUNDAY 3rd JUNE 1951

A Doug Cowie penalty gives Dundee a 1-0 win over Hapoel in Tel Aviv in their second game of their tour of Israel and Turkey. Five days later The Dee would face a combined Hapoel and Maccabi side and suffered the first reverse of the tour with a 2-1 defeat.

## SUNDAY 3rd JUNE 1962

After training in Central Park, Dundee win their first game in the New York Tourney when they defeat Guadalajara of Mexico 3-2 thanks to goals from Andy Penman (2) and Alan Gilzean. Scotland normally sent over the league runners-up to the competition and with Rangers resurgent in the spring, the Scottish League nominated

Dundee as its representative. But with Dundee fighting back to win the title on the last day of the season, it was the champions of Scotland, rather than the runners-up, who took part for the first and only time and it caused much consternation at the SFA. Dundee received some unexpected backing from 70 Scots brought down from Canada by ex-Celtic goalkeeper Joe Kennaway and the ex-pats were introduced to Bob Shankly and thanked for their support after the win.

## SUNDAY 4th JUNE 1967

Dundee draw 2-2 with Chelsea in Miami in the last game of their North American tour with the goals coming from Sammy Wilson and Jocky Scott. Scott finished the tour with 11 goals in 11 games.

## THURSDAY 5th JUNE 1924

Goals from Davie McLean and Charlie Duncan help Dundee defeat Barcelona for the second time in five days at their Camp de les Corts with a 2-1 win on their tour of Spain. After the match Davie Halliday received the horrendous news of his two-year-old son's death through a scalding accident at his home in Dumfries and immediately prepared to return home.

## SATURDAY 6th JUNE 1953

Dundee continued to knock in the goals in South Africa with a 4-0 win over Western Province in Cape Town with strikes from Bobby Flavell, Ronnie Turnbull and Bert Henderson (2). With the Dundee party moving to a different location for every match in their first month in South Africa, they were given a fantastic opportunity to experience and visit the whole country.

## SUNDAY 7th JUNE 1959

An Alan Cousin goal gives Dundee a 1-0 win over a Chicago XI in front of 7,000 on their North American tour. Dundee had sailed out on the SS Mauretania on May 6th and returned by air after their last game which was a 3-3 draw with Legia Warsaw of Poland in New York on June 14th.

## SUNDAY 8th JUNE 1924

Real Madrid were looking for revenge for the previous year's losses to Dundee when they met in a two-day double header but they turned out to both be ill-tempered games. With Dundee leading 1-0 in the first match, the game exploded when the Spanish referee, who had officiated from the shade in the stand with a lemon in his hand, awarded Real a dubious penalty. The Dundee players were incensed by this and when the referee came from under his cover and placed the ball on the spot, an exasperated Willie Rankine kicked it into the net. At this, the official tried to slap Rankine in the face but he was quickly pushed away by the Dundee centre-half who was then sent off for his trouble. At first he refused to go and so six armed policeman tried to intervene but when he shook them off, the entire Dundee team walked off in protest. There was uproar amongst the 6,000 crowd and it looked as though the police would have to worry more about the crowd than the conduct of Rankine. After the intervention of Dundee manager Sandy MacFarlane and treasurer Willie McIntosh, the game continued after they persuaded their players to take to the field again and was played out to a 1-1 draw.

## MONDAY 9th JUNE 1924

Twenty-four hours later double the number of fans turned up for 'round two' of Real Madrid v Dundee, attended by the royalty of both Italy and Spain. They witnessed a very satisfying 2-1 win for The Dee thanks to goals from Charlie Duncan and Crawford Letham but the game was marred again by rough play with Jock Gilmour and a Spanish defender both dismissed in separate incidents.

## TUESDAY 10th JUNE 1947

In front of a crowd of 10,000 Dundee defeat a Zeeland XI 5-2 on their tour of Denmark and Sweden. Ernie Ewen and Albert Juliussen both netted a double with Johnny Pattillo also on the score sheet.

## SUNDAY 10th JUNE 1962

Suffering from heat exhaustion Gordon Smith flew home before Dundee's match with Italian side Palermo in the New York Tourney but promised to fly back if the Dark Blues win their qualifying group. However, the match finished 1-1 with Bobby Waddell getting the Dundee goal and it means The Dee can't now win the section with just one game to go.

## WEDNESDAY 11th JUNE 1986

For the third tour match in a row, Graham Harvey is on target to give Dundee a 1-0 win over Orlando in the penultimate match of their tour of the USA and Canada. Harvey had scored in the two wins over Seattle Storm and FC Portland over the past five days which both finished 2-1 to The Dee.

## MONDAY 12th JUNE 1893

Dundee, Cowlairs, Hibernian and St Bernards formally apply to join the Scottish League at their AGM alongside the bottom three sides, Renton, Abercorn and Clyde who were applying for re-election. It is Dundee, Renton and St Bernards who are successful, meaning the former office bearers of Our Boys and East End can now appoint office bearers for the newly formed Dundee Football and Athletic Club and start to plan for their first ever season.

## SATURDAY 13th JUNE 1953

Dundee played the eighth game of their South African tour when they met Eastern Transvaal at Willowmere Park, Benoni near Johannesburg. Goals from Billy Steel, Bobby Flavell (2) and George Christie give the tourists a 4-2 win.

## THURSDAY 13th JUNE 1985

Playing on Astroturf, Dundee defeat Portland 7-0 on their tour of the USA and Canada. It's a comfortable win for the Dark Blues against opposition of poor quality, who are no relation to the Major League Soccer club Portland Timbers. The win is secured by goals from John McCormack (2), Graham Harvey (2), Bobby Glennie, Robert Connor and Derek McWilliams.

## SUNDAY 14th JUNE 1953

Dundee fly 500 miles to Lourenco Marques in Portuguese East Africa to play their second game in 24 hours. Against a Lourenco Marques XI, goals from Bobby Flavell and Doug Cowie give The Dee a 3-1 win and had it not been for the heroics of local goalkeeper Costa Pereira, who made a series of spectacular saves, the score could have been a lot higher.

## SATURDAY 14th JUNE 1986

Dundee face English side Queens Park Rangers in Tampa in the USA and a Robert Connor goal earns the Dark Blues a 1-1 draw in the final match of their North American tour.

## SUNDAY 15th JUNE 1924

Dundee moved to the Galicia province for the first of a triple header against Deportivo La Coruña on their tour of Spain. The match report says the whole town turned up to see the game and a Davie McLean hat-trick earns The Dee a 3-3 draw. The Dark Blues would end their Spanish adventure with a defeat (1-5) and a win (2-0) against Deportivo.

## SUNDAY 15th JUNE 1958

Dundee's Doug Cowie is dropped after playing in the first two World Cup finals matches against Yugoslavia (1-1) and Paraguay (2-3) but goalkeeper Bill Brown makes his Scotland debut in the final group match against France in Sweden. Brown would win four of his 28 Scotland caps while at Dens Park and his appearance in the 2-1 defeat in Orebro was the last time a Dundee player played in the World Cup finals.

## WEDNESDAY 16th JUNE 1954

Doug Cowie becomes the first Dundee player to play in the World Cup finals when he lines up for Scotland against Austria in a 1-0 defeat in Zurich in Switzerland. Cowie would play in two matches in both the 1954 and 1958 World Cups amongst his 20 Scotland caps and is the second most capped Dee of all time behind Alex Hamilton.

## SATURDAY 16th JUNE 1962

Dundee lose 3-2 to eventual Section One winners FC America in their last game of the New York Tourney with the consolation strikes coming from forwards Bobby Waddell and Alan Gilzean. The Dee finished fifth in their six team group with a record of P5, W1, D2, L2, GF9, GA11, Pts 4. FC America went on to defeat Section 2 winners Belenenses of Portugal 3-1 on aggregate, thereby wining the 1962 New York International Tourney without losing a game, but they would then lose 3-2 on aggregate to 1961 winners Dukla Prague in a play-off for the American Challenge Cup.

## SATURDAY 16th JUNE 2001

There is little break for the Dundee squad as the club opted to take part in the Uefa Intertoto Cup just four weeks after their last SPL match. Drawn against FK Sartid of Yugoslavia in the first round, with the winners due to meet 1860 Munich in the second, it is Dundee's first foray into Europe since 1974. In front of a crowd of 6,500 on a beautiful sunny day, Dundee and Sartid draw 0-0 in a somewhat surreal atmosphere in the first leg.

## MONDAY 17th JUNE 1946

Dundee played the British Territorial Army for the third time on their tour of West Germany, Austria and Italy and win 6-2 in Vienna. The match is played in the 80,000 capacity Prater Stadium, described as 'Hampden-like in its dimensions' and Peter Rattray and Reggie Smith delight the 10,000 crowd with their play on the left. The win is secured thanks to goals from Albert Juliussen (3), Reggie Smith, Peter Rattray and Johnny Pattillo.

## SUNDAY 17th JUNE 1951

Hat-tricks from Bobby Flavell and Ernie Copland gives Dundee a 6-0 win over Galatasaray in front of a crowd of 8,000 in Istanbul in the first of a double header. Galatasaray get revenge with a 2-1 win six days later.

## TUESDAY 18th JUNE 1985

Dundee defeat Edmonton Brick Men 5-1 on the final game of their tour of USA and Canada. In front of a 2,436 crowd, Dundee's goals come from five different scorers, namely Jim Smith, Ray Stephen, George McGeachie, Graham Harvey and John McCormack.

## FRIDAY 19th JUNE 1953

Dundee faced the Orange Free State in Bloemfontein on their South African tour. Doug Cowie has to leave the field with 15 minutes left through injury but it doesn't stop The Dee winning 9-2 thanks to goals from Ronnie Turnbull (3), George Christie (2), Billy Steel (2), Bobby Flavell and Bert Walker.

## SATURDAY 20th JUNE 1953

Doug Cowie recovers to face Northern Transvaal in Pretoria 24 hours later and goals from George Hill and Bert Henderson give the tartan clad Dee a 2-0 win.

## FRIDAY 21st JUNE 2013

Gavin Rae rejoined Dundee for a third time and is appointed club captain by manager John Brown. He would go on to play in every game in the SPFL Championship winning season and would lift the trophy on the final day after a 2-1 win over Dumbarton at Dens. Rae would hang up his boots in the aftermath, leaving a Dark Blue legacy of 303 appearances and 32 goals.

## SATURDAY 22nd JUNE 1963

Fifteen-year-old Jocky Scott joins Dundee from Chelsea to start a Dark Blue love affair that would last on and off for the next 46 years. Scott's 433 appearances, including a League Cup final win over Celtic in 1973 and three spells as manager, see him rightly sit among the club's elite and he was inducted into the inaugural Dundee FC Hall of Fame in 2009 with a Legends Award.

## TUESDAY 23rd JUNE 1953

Dundee defeat Southern Transvaal 4-0 in a floodlit game in the Rand Stadium in Johannesburg. It was one of the coldest nights of the year so only 10,000, half the ground's capacity, braved the weather and they witness goals from Billy Steel, Ken Ziesing and George Christie (2) in their toughest test of their South African tour so far.

## SATURDAY 23rd JUNE 2001

Mindful of the NATO airstrikes on Belgrade during the Kosovo conflict two years previously, the Foreign Office advised Dundee not to travel to Serbia for the second leg of the Uefa Intertoto Cup first round match with FK Sartid. Fabian Caballero gave Dundee the lead after four minutes when he cleverly chested home a headflick by Gavin Rae. However, in a three-minute spell, Sartid twice converted questionable penalty awards and made it 3-1 just before half-time. Juan Sara reduced the deficit on the hour when he headed home a

BILLY STEEL LOOKS RESPLENDENT IN THE ANDERSON TARTAN SHIRT ON DUNDEE'S TOUR OF SOUTH AFRICA

fine run and cross by Caballero but with 15 minutes left Caballero was sent off for retaliation after some brutal treatment. Sartid scored twice more to send The Dee home with 5-2 defeat thus ending their brief foray into Europe.

### SUNDAY 24th JUNE 1951

In the final game of their tour of Israel and Turkey, Dundee draw 2-2 with an Istanbul Select which comprised players from Besiktas, Galatasaray and Fenerbahçe. In front of a crowd of 10,000 the Dark Blues' goals were scored by Ernie Ewen and Bobby Flavell.

### THURSDAY 25th JUNE 2009

Leigh Griffiths joined Dundee from Livingston for a £125,000 fee and would become a popular player in his two seasons at Dens. 'Sparky' scored 29 goals in 56 appearances, won the Scottish League Challenge Cup and was a Dee-Fiant hero before being sold to Wolverhampton Wanderers for £150,000 by Administrator Bryan Jackson in January 2011.

### WEDNESDAY 26th JUNE 1947

On a scorching hot afternoon in Trieste, Italy, Albert Juliussen scores four as Dundee defeat the British Territorial Army 13th Corp 5-1. The poetically named Kinnaird Ouchterlonie scores Dundee's other goal in the last game of their tour of West Germany, Austria and Italy playing army sides.

### SATURDAY 27th JUNE 1953

In the first of a three match test series against the South African national team, Dundee lose 1-0 in Durban; their first and only defeat on the tour.

### TUESDAY 28th JUNE 2016

Dundee play their first pre-season game of the 2016/17 campaign at The Cheaper Insurance Direct Stadium against Dumbarton. A double from Cammy Kerr gives The Dee a 2-1 win. Mark O'Hara, Danny Williams and Yordi Teijsse make their Dark Blue debuts after joining the club in the summer and the sides would meet again a month later in a League Cup group match at Dens which The Dee won 6-2.

## MONDAY 29th JUNE 2009

Dundee announced that Viga Athletic Clothing and Bukta Teamwear will be the club shirt sponsors for season 2009/10. They are owned by the same parent company and, for the first time in the club's history, the home and away shirts would have different sponsors on them, with Viga on the dark blue home shirt and Bukta on the white away shirt.

## MONDAY 30th JUNE 2014

Fan favourite and Dee-Fiant captain Gary Harkins rejoined Dundee for a third time from St Mirren, after spending the second half of the previous season at Oldham Athletic. His third spell would see him turn out 66 times, scoring 9 goals, before departing for Ayr United on August 12th 2016. His Dark Blue career yielded a total of 33 goals in 160 appearances. The Dundee support will be forever grateful to 'Jeebsy' for the part he played in helping save the club as skipper when the club went into administration in 2010.

# DUNDEE FC
## *On This Day*

## JULY

## WEDNESDAY 1st JULY 1953

Billy Steel misses the game with tonsillitis but Doug Cowie scores a hat-trick as Dundee win 4-1 in the first of their two games against Southern Rhodesia in Salisbury. Cowie opens the scoring in six minutes when he sends a scorching shot into the net. His second comes two minutes after the break when he hammers the ball home from 20 yards and completes his hat-trick four minutes later when he pokes home a goalmouth scramble. Albert Henderson makes it 4-0 before Tilley scores a consolation.

## WEDNESDAY 2nd JULY 1919

Dundee's longest serving manager William Wallace steps down after 20 years service after joining Dundee as secretary and taking over team affairs in 1899. Three times he led Dundee to runners-up in the Scottish League Championship in the early part of the 20th century but his greatest triumph was winning the Scottish Cup in 1910 with victory over Clyde at Ibrox; The Dee's first major trophy. In total he takes charge for 684 games and stands down as the Dark Blues resume after a one-year closure towards the end of the First World War.

## MONDAY 3rd JULY 1944

George Anderson joins the new Dundee FC board of directors as the club prepares to resume after going into abeyance in 1940 and becomes manager of the team. His post-war time in charge from 1944 to 1955 is the most successful era in the Dark Blues' history. 'Toffee Dod' as he was nicknamed, led Dundee to back-to-back League Cup wins in 1951 and 1952. He also wins two Scottish League B Division titles in a row and finishes runner-up in the Scottish League Championship in 1949 and the Scottish Cup in 1952. He is inducted into the club's Hall of Fame in 2013 with a Heritage Award.

## SATURDAY 4th JULY 1953

Turning on the heat from the first whistle, Dundee run riot against Southern Rhodesia at the Queen's Ground, Bulawayo. The tourists lead 5-0 at the break thanks to goals from George Christie (2), Jack Cowan, Ronnie Turnbull and Doug Cowie with the Rhodesians unable to find an answer to the sparkling link-up between the forwards and the wing-halves, Andy Irvine and Jackie Stewart. Dundee bring on

Bobby Flavell and Billy Steel at half time and Flavell gets a brace and Steel also scores as The Dee win 8-0.

## WEDNESDAY 5th JULY 1899

The old main stand at Carolina Port is dismantled to be reassembled at Dundee's new ground at Dens Park which is due to be opened for the new season. Dens Park will be Dundee's third home ground in six years after West Craigie Park and Carolina Port.

## THURSDAY 6th JULY 1961

Thirty-seven-year-old Gordon Smith makes his debut for Dundee after joining on a free transfer from Hearts. He scores alongside Bobby Waddell and Andy Penman as Dundee defeat KR Reykjavik 3-1 in the first game of their pre-season tour of Iceland.

## SATURDAY 7th JULY 2012

Dundee proved too hot to handle for Lancaster City as two goals either side of half-time ensure a perfect start to their pre-season. Ryan Conroy gave Dundee the lead after 15 minutes when the ex-Celtic kid has the ball in the net, albeit with the help of the Dolly Blues' captain Neil Marshall who heads Conroy's wicked cross into his own net. Dundee are pegged back with five minutes of the first half remaining as Zac Clark cuts in from the left to slot past Rab Douglas but Barry Smith's side show their mettle after the break and earn their just reward when Stephen O'Donnell pops up to bag a deserved winner.

## WEDNESDAY 8th JULY 2015

Dundee are on day three of their pre-season training camp at the Globall Football Park in Hungary which Paul Hartley's squad has travelled to for the second year in a row.

## SUNDAY 9th JULY 1961

Dundee face Icelandic champions Akranes who have eight internationalists in their side and win 4-0 in the second game on their tour of Iceland. The goals come from Alan Cousin, Andy Penman (2) and Gordon Smith whose second goal in two games excites former Dee Tommy Gallagher reporting for The Courier, while the local press describe Dundee as, 'Apart from Dynamo Moscow, the best side ever to play on Iceland.'

## SATURDAY 10th JULY 2010

Gordon Chisholm's Dundee and Milton Keynes Dons draw 0-0 in a closed door pre-season friendly at Dens. It is Karl Robinson's first game in charge of MK Dons after he took over as manager from Paul Ince in May after serving as his assistant.

## SATURDAY 11th JULY 1953

Dundee gain revenge in the second test against South Africa at the Rand Stadium in Johannesburg with an impressive 5-0 win. Bobby Flavell scores a hat-trick with his third described by the local press as 'the best ever scored at South Africa's largest soccer ground' when he beats four men and walks round the amazed keeper before tapping the ball over the line. Ronnie Turnbull and Ken Ziesing complete the rout.

## WEDNESDAY 12th JULY 1961

Dundee complete their schedule in Iceland by defeating an Iceland Select 3-1 thanks to goals from Alan Gilzean and Hugh Robertson (2). The game is remembered for the referee pushing newly appointed Dundee skipper Bobby Cox in the chest after he queries a decision. Cox walks off the field thinking he has been sent off but it transpires afterwards that he had only been issued with a reprimand.

## SUNDAY 13th JULY 2014

On the same day as the World Cup final in Rio, English champions Manchester City come to Dens for a pre-season friendly and Manuel Pellegrini fields a side worth £165m against the SPFL Championship winners. Wearing their pre-season red kit, Dundee take the lead on 27 minutes when Gary Harkins hits home the rebound after City debutant Willy Caballero saves his initial penalty after a foul by Jason Denayer. German trialist Luka Tankulic adds a second 11 minutes later, converting a cross from Harkins with the help of a deflection off defender Dedryck Boyata to give The Dee a memorable 2-0 win.

## SATURDAY 14th JULY 2007

New signing 6'7" Czech striker Jan Zemlik makes his home debut in a pre-season friendly against English Football League Championship side Millwall at Dens and scores a double as the Dark Blues win 2-1.

CHAMPIONS V CHAMPIONS! SPFL CHAMPIONSHIP WINNERS DUNDEE LINE UP TO FACE ENGLISH PREMIER LEAGUE CHAMPIONS MANCHESTER CITY AT DENS

## WEDNESDAY 15th JULY 1953

Dundee beat South Africa 5-3 at Hartleyvale, Cape Town to win the test series by two games to one. It is the final match of their 17-game tour where they won 15, drew 1 and lost 1. For the first time in Africa, Dundee play on a rain-soaked pitch after heavy rain fell before the game. Ronnie Turnbull opens the scoring on 14 minutes when the referee overrules the linesman who had flagged for offside. Doug Cowie scores the second but Dundee protest when the Springboks score after right winger Claasens sends in a fierce angled shot which hits the post, but the referee rules it had gone over the line. South Africa then equalise through Keys before the break but Turnbull restores Dundee's lead two minutes after the restart. Billy Steel gets The Dee's fourth before Keys pulls another one back, but two minutes from time Ken Ziesing heads home a Billy Steel free kick to secure the victory.

## SATURDAY 16th JULY 2011

Dundee defeat Paul Sturrock's Southend United 2-0 at Bayview in the Gilvenbank Hotel Football Festival thanks to goals from Graham Bayne and Graham Webster. The following day Dundee meet East Fife, who beat Raith Rovers in the other semi-final. The hosts beat The Dee 1-0 to win the tournament and lift the trophy.

## MONDAY 16th JULY 2012

Due to the demise of Glasgow Rangers, it is agreed at an SPL board meeting that Dundee FC would be invited to be 'Club 12' for the 2012/13 season in the Clydesdale Bank Premier League. With the league kicking off on the 4th August, this gives Dundee just 19 days to prepare for life in the top flight after spending all summer building a team for the First Division.

## TUESDAY 17th JULY 1984

Dundee draw 1-1 with Borussia Dortmund on the first game of their tour of West Germany and Switzerland. Colin Harris gets Dundee's goal in the Westfalenstadion.

## WEDNESDAY 18th JULY 1984

Just 24 hours later Dundee face SV Gottingen 05 on their tour of West Germany and Switzerland. They win 5-1 thanks to goals from Stuart Rafferty, Trialist, John Brown, Lex Richardson and Tosh McKinlay.

## SATURDAY 19th JULY 2014

Dundee win 4-2 at Morecambe's Globe Arena in a pre-season friendly as they prepare for life back in the top flight. Wearing their pre-season red kit again, Dundee's goals come from Kieron Cadogan, Gary Harkins, Martin Boyle and Peter MacDonald. Cadogan is on trial and despite scoring doesn't do enough to impress manager Paul Hartley and win a contract.

## MONDAY 20th JULY 1992

Dundee defeat Deveronvale 4-1 in a pre-season friendly in Banff. Canadian striker Alex Bunberry scores a hat-trick with centre-half Willie Jamieson also on target. Dundee manager Simon Stainrod had hoped to sign Bunberry permanently but with only ten non-European Community players allowed in the Premier Division and nine permits already allocated, Dundee lose out to Celtic who obtain clearance for Albanian internationalist Rudi Vata.

## SUNDAY 21st JULY 1996

After losing 2-1 to York City the day before, Dundee defeat Queens Park 4-2 in the 3rd/4th play-off in the Livingston FC Tournament at Almondvale. Paul Tosh (2), Jim Hamilton and Iain Anderson get the goals that defeat The Spiders.

## TUESDAY 22nd JULY 1975

Dundee start their tour of Sweden with a 4-0 win over IFK Oestersund in front of a crowd of 6,000 at the Hofvallens IP Stadium. Dundee's goals are scored by Jocky Scott, Bobby Robinson, Gordon Wallace and Alan Gordon.

## SATURDAY 23rd JULY 2011

In the first game after the Dee-Fiant season, Dundee open the new campaign with a Scottish League Challenge Cup tie with Arbroath at Gayfield. Jordan Elfverson gives the Red Litchies the lead on 77 minutes but two minutes later Steven Milne equalises to take the tie into extra time. Steven O'Donnell scores within two minutes of the restart to send the Dark Blues through.

## TUESDAY 24th JULY 1984

Dundee defeat Horgen 11-0 in Switzerland thanks to goals from Colin Harris (2), Ray Stephen (2), Colin Hendry (2), Gerry Docherty (2), Bobby Glennie, Tosh McKinlay and Lex Richardson.

## SATURDAY 24th JULY 2010

Dundee opened their season with a Scottish League Challenge Cup tie with Alloa Athletic at Dens. It looks like Gordon Chisholm's new side might be heading out after Scott Walker gave The Wasps the lead on 74 minutes but two goals in the last six minutes from Colin McMenamin and Sean Higgins sees The Dee sneak through.

## FRIDAY 24th JULY 2015

After joining on a pre-contract agreement from Falkirk, Rory Loy scores his first Dundee goal in a pre-season friendly with Gary Caldwell's Wigan Athletic at Dens. Despite a dominant performance from The Latics, watched by 200 of their fans, Loy's 70th strike into the bottom right hand corner is enough for a 1-0 win. Caldwell and Dundee manger Paul Hartley had been teammates together at Celtic where they won two SPL titles, one Scottish Cup and one League Cup together and lined up in the same Scotland side 13 times.

## WEDNESDAY 24th JULY 1984

There are two hat-tricks from Dundee players as they defeat Eppstein 9-1 on their tour of West Germany and Switzerland. Albert Kidd scores four and Walker McCall three with the other goals coming from Tosh McKinlay and John Docherty. Docherty would make just one substitute appearance in a competitive match for The Dee in a 2-1 defeat to Dumbarton at Boghead a month later.

## FRIDAY 25th JULY 1975

Twenty-four hours after defeating IFK Oskashamn 5-1 on their tour of Sweden, Dundee beat Soelversburg 3-1. The goals are scored by George Stewart and Gordon Wallace (2) and two days later the Dark Blues would conclude their trip with a 3-2 victory at IFK Ystad.

## SUNDAY 25th JULY 2004

Dundee hansel the new Falkirk Stadium and compete for the Slater-Merchant Trophy (named after Bert Slater and George Merchant who both won the Scottish Cup with Falkirk and played for Dundee). The Dark Blues lift the trophy with a 2-0 win over The Bairns thanks to a double from new signing John Sutton who has just joined on a year-long loan from Millwall.

## SATURDAY 26th JULY 1980

A Jimmy Murphy goal earns Dundee a 1-1 draw at Torquay United in a pre-season friendly in front of a 1,454 crowd at Plainmoor. It is former Dundee United goalkeeper Donald McKay's first game in charge after taking over from Tommy Gemmell in the summer.

## SATURDAY 27th JULY 2013

Dundee open their season with a Scottish League Challenge Cup tie against Paul Hartley's Alloa Athletic at Recreation Park. Hartley had led The Wasps into the SPFL Championship after two successive promotions but Carlo Monti's 59th minute penalty past Scott Bain is enough to see the Dark Blues into the second round.

## TUESDAY 28th JULY 1960

Bobby Seith signs for Dundee from Burnley for a fee over £7,500 just after winning the English League title with the Turf Moor side. Two years later he would win the Scottish equivalent with Dundee and would captain the Dark Blues in the 1963 European Cup semi-final against AC Milan in the absence of the injured Bobby Cox. Seith would later coach at Dens and was inducted into the Dundee Hall of Fame in 2012 with a Legends Award.

## SATURDAY 28th JULY 2001

Dundee start their league campaign at Tannadice with a 2-2 draw against Dundee United. Charlie Miller hits the bar with a penalty but makes amends for the home side when he gives The Arabs the lead nine minutes later. Juan Sara draws Dundee level within two minutes before Gavin Rae gives the Dark Blues the lead but a dramatic injury-time equaliser from ex-Dee Jim Hamilton means a share of the points.

## SATURDAY 29th JULY 2000

Two thousand Dees travel to Fir Park to watch Ivano Bonetti's first game in charge at Motherwell in the opening game of the season. An eighth minute goal from Patrizio Billio sets the scene for an exhilarating first half display in which Dundee hit the woodwork three times. Bonetti is sent off soon after the restart for a second yellow card but the Dark Blues withstand the Motherwell pressure and with four minutes left Javier Artero completes a dazzling dribble past five home players to fire home a decisive second.

## SATURDAY 30th JULY 2011

Dundee travel to the Bet Butler Stadium to take on Dumbarton in the first round of the Scottish League Cup. Barry Smith's side are dominant throughout and progress with a 4-0 win thanks to goals from Stevie Milne (2), Jamie McClusky and a Matt Lockwood penalty.

## WEDNESDAY 31st JULY 2013

Dundee celebrate their 120th anniversary with a special commemorative challenge match at Dens Park against Rangers who they had faced in their first ever match. Declan Gallagher gives Dundee the lead, heading home a Nicky Riley corner, but Honduran Arnold Peralta equalises with a stunning free kick and the match finishes level, just as it had done in 1893.

# DUNDEE FC
## *On This Day*

# AUGUST

## TUESDAY 1st AUGUST 1893

Dundee's first ever captain William 'Plum' Longair officially signs from East End to start almost 30 years of service to the club as player and trainer. As a player Longair lined up in Dundee's first ever game against Rangers 12 days later, makes 136 appearances and wins one Scotland cap. As trainer he is part of the 1910 Scottish Cup winning side and is inducted into the club's inaugural Hall of Fame in 2009 with a Heritage Award.

## SATURDAY 1st AUGUST 2015

Dundee begin their season and storm to the top of the SPFL Premiership with a sensational 4-0 win at Kilmarnock. Greg Stewart gives Dundee the lead when he lashes home a 20-yard drive before Rory Loy doubles the lead just before the break, converting a Kevin Holt cross. Debutant Loy nets again early in the second period when he heads home an audacious Gary Harkins lob from the touchline and Stewart rounds off a superb day with a late fourth.

## SATURDAY 2nd AUGUST 1997

Dundee start their Scottish League First Division winning campaign with a 3-0 home win over 1997 Scottish Cup runners-up Falkirk. On a warm, sunny day over 4,500 turn up to watch Jerry O'Driscoll power home the opener before Eddie Annand adds a second on the hour. Just before full time, 17-year-old substitute John Elliot fires home a penalty to give Dundee the perfect start to the season.

## SATURDAY 3rd AUGUST 2002

With Jim Duffy back in charge for a third spell, Dundee begin a memorable season with a 1-1 home draw with Heart of Midlothian. In front of just under 8,000 at Dens, Dundee dominate and attack at every opportunity with their adventurous 4-3-3 system and Fabian Caballero scores a cracking goal to earn the draw.

## SATURDAY 4th AUGUST 2012

Dundee return to the top flight for the first time in seven years as 'Club 12' with a 0-0 draw at Kilmarnock. When Rangers are demoted to the fourth tier after liquidating and reforming, the SPL publish their fixtures listing a 'Club 12' which they later announce as Dundee FC who had finished as First Division runners-up. In the first game of the season the Dark Blues travel to Rugby Park and over 2,500 Dees journey to Ayrshire to see Dundee earn a point which could have been more had new signing John Baird not passed up a good chance.

## SATURDAY 5th AUGUST 1944

Two months after the D-Day landings, 14,000 turn up to Dens to watch Dundee return to action after being closed for the Second World War. They face a British Army side which includes household names like Frank Swift, Joe Mercer, and Matt Busby and it is no disgrace to lose 7-0 to a near international XI.

## SATURDAY 6th AUGUST 2011

Dundee travel to Firhill to face Partick Thistle in the opening game of the Scottish League First Division season. It is a tight, dour game but after Nicky Riley is brought down in the box in the 90th minute, Matt Lockwood hits home the penalty to give Dundee a 1-0 win in front of 3,065 spectators.

## SATURDAY 7th AUGUST 2010

In what would be the first league game of the Dee-Fiant season, Queen of the South visit Dens and debutant Netan Sansara, signed the day before, is sent off after 70 minutes. Just four minutes later, Dundee are down to nine men when Nicky Riley is also sent off but, for the remaining quarter of an hour, the players show a desire and spirit that they would become famed for later that season. Already 1-0 ahead through new captain Gary Harkins' first half goal, The Dee do well to see the game out as the Dumfries side throws everything at the nine men. Robert Douglas had already saved a penalty just before Sansara's dismissal and the players work tirelessly to close down their opponents with Rhys Weston and Craig McKeown immense at the back.

## SATURDAY 8th AUGUST 1953

Bobby Flavell scores four and Billy Steel two as defending champions Dundee start their season with a 6-1 sectional League Cup win over Stirling Albion at Dens. The holders would fail to qualify from their section when they lose their last game 4-0 to Partick Thistle in front of 30,000 at Firhill and would be knocked out on goal average with nine points. A 3-0 defeat would have been enough to see The Dee through.

## WEDNESDAY 8th AUGUST 1979

Dundee knock Kilmarnock out of the Anglo-Scottish Cup on away goals after a 3-3 draw at Rugby Park. A Jim Shirra strike earns Dundee a 1-1 draw at Dens two days before and goals from Eric Sinclair and Ian Redford (2) make the aggregate score 4-4 but it is enough to see the Dark Blues through.

## SATURDAY 9th AUGUST 1952

The by now traditional League Cup seasonal opener is the first match of the 1952/53 season with Dundee facing Raith Rovers at Dens. It is the first match in the defence of the trophy they had won at Hampden the previous year and they kick off in the white kit they had worn in the Scottish Cup final in April. It is the first time therefore that a club badge has been worn in a match at Dens and a healthy crowd of 20,000 turn up for the new campaign to watch Dundee win 2-1 thanks to goals from Gerry Burrell and Billy Steel.

## SATURDAY 9th AUGUST 2014

Dundee unveil their SPFL Championship winning flag before a 1-1 draw with Kilmarnock in the first game of the Scottish Premiership season. Dundee mark their return to the top flight by sharing the spoils with Killie and it is their former player Gary Harkins who wins and then converts a penalty to give The Dee the lead. It lasts less than ten minutes when Craig Slater hits home a superb free kick.

## SATURDAY 10th AUGUST 1991

Dundee begin their First Division winning campaign with five straight wins, the first of which is a 2-1 win over Clydebank at Kilbowie. The goals come from Albert Craig and Duncan Campbell and Craig would score seven goals in the first six games and then just two more the rest of the season.

## SATURDAY 11th AUGUST 1973

Dundee open their successful League Cup campaign with a 1-0 home win over St Johnstone with fullback Bobby Wilson netting the winner. The Dee would qualify out of their section ahead of the Perth side with 10 points from the six group games.

## TUESDAY 11th AUGUST 2015

A James McPake 94th minute goal sees Dundee come back from 2-0 down to draw 2-2 with Dundee United at Tannadice. Blair Spittal appears to shatter The Dee's hopes with two second-half goals but with nine minutes left Greg Stewart hits a beautiful curling effort into the top left-hand corner from the edge of the box to give the Dark Blues hope. As the game moves into injury time Scott Bain somehow gets his fingertips to Scott Murray's shot to tip it onto the underside of the bar before Dundee go up the park to equalise. A United clearance falls to Charlie Telfer 30 yards out but he is robbed by Gary Harkins who hits a long range effort at goal. Goalkeeper Zwick can only push the ball away and McPake slides in to score and send the Dundee fans wild with delight.

## SATURDAY 12th AUGUST 1893

For Dundee FC it truly is 'The Glorious Twelfth' as they play their first ever match against Rangers at West Craigie Park. After falling two goals behind, inside-left Sandy Gilligan scores Dundee's first ever goal. This sparks a revival in which Sandy Keillor and Jimmy Dundas put Dundee 3-2 ahead but before the end, Rangers' John Gray completes both his hat-trick and the scoring for the game. 'Thus has Dundee been successfully launched on its League career,' comments *The Advertiser* and the fledgling homesters can be well pleased with their 3-3 draw.

## SATURDAY 12th AUGUST 1972

In the opening game of the season John Duncan creates a new club record for most goals in a League Cup match when he scores five against East Stirlingshire at Firs Park. Further goals from Bobby Robinson, Jimmy Wilson and an own goal from Bobby Stein give the Dark Blues an 8-2 win in the sectional tie.

## SATURDAY 12th AUGUST 1961

Dundee's championship-winning season gets off to a flyer when Bobby Wishart scores after just three minutes against Airdrieonians at Dens in a sectional League Cup tie. The 13,000 crowd has to wait until the second half for Alan Cousin to net the clincher from close range to give The Dee a 2-0 win.

## SATURDAY 13th AUGUST 1994

Having been relegated from the Premier Division at the end of the previous season, Dundee start their First Division campaign with a 2-0 home win over St Mirren thanks to goals from strikers George Shaw and Gerry Britton.

## THURSDAY 14th AUGUST 2003

Dundee's first premier European match in 29 years is a tricky Uefa Cup preliminary round tie with KS Vllaznia in Shkoder but The Dee come back from Albania in the first leg with a 2-0 win. Just 100 diehard Dees make the trip after British Embassy security concerns and although Vllaznia are useful enough in possession, the Dark Blues settle quickly before an 11,000 crowd in the Loro Borici Stadium. In 41 minutes Steve Lovell gives Dundee a priceless away goal and another strike from Nacho Novo in the second half ensures it was a suitably triumphant Euro return. Dundee are the first Scottish side to win in Albania; a feat that neither Celtic's Lisbon Lions nor Aberdeen's Gothenburg Greats could achieve in their trophy winning European campaigns.

## WEDNESDAY 15th AUGUST 1962

Dundee expected a home match to open the 1962/63 season to unfurl their Scottish League champions flag but have to wait until the second game in a midweek League Cup sectional tie with Celtic. Lady Provost McManus raises the flag on a specially erected post behind the goal at the TC Keay end in which Gordon Smith scores a 60th-minute goal to give the Dark Blues a 1-0 win.

## SATURDAY 15th AUGUST 1992

With player-manager Simon Stainrod resplendent in the dugout wearing his ankle length raincoat and fedora hat, Dundee defeat Rangers 4-3 at Dens. First, Dutchman Ivo Den Biemen then Ian Gilzean put Dundee in front with headed goals only for Ally McCoist to twice bring Rangers level. Just after the hour Billy Dodds restores Dundee's lead when he sweeps home Gilzean's knock-on before Iain Ferguson makes it 3-3 with ten minutes to go. Dundee weren't to be denied however and when Gilzean is impeded in the box by Richard Gough, Billy Dodds converts the penalty to give the newly-promoted Dee a famous 4-3 win over the reigning champions.

## SUNDAY 15th AUGUST 2004

Dundee cross the road to Tannadice and return with a 2-1 derby win over Dundee United in front of a live TV audience. Steve Lovell gives the Dark Blues the lead from the spot after the returning Iain Anderson is downed in the box and just after the break Lovell crosses for fellow Englishman John Sutton to net at the front post to set The Dee on the road to victory.

## SATURDAY 16th AUGUST 1958

Ian Ure signs for Dundee from Ayr Albion and four years later is a key man in Dundee's Scottish League title success and run to the European Cup semi-final the following year. The centre-half makes 146 appearances for The Dee, is named Scottish Player of the Year for 1962 and is inducted into the club's Hall of Fame in 2011 with a Legends Award.

## SATURDAY 16th AUGUST 1997

Goals from Eddie Annand, James Grady and Lee Maddison give Dundee a 3-0 win away at Partick Thistle in their First Division winning campaign. It is Grady and Maddison's first goals for the club and Grady would finish the season as top goalscorer with 18 and would win the SPFA First Division Player of the Year title.

## SATURDAY 17th AUGUST 2013

Dundee start their Scottish Championship winning campaign with a 1-0 win over Paul Hartley's Alloa Athletic at Dens but it takes a 93rd minute penalty winner from Kevin McBride who slots it home past Scott Bain with the last kick of the match.

## MONDAY 18th AUGUST 1917

With Dundee placed into the Scottish League North-Eastern Division to minimise the travelling of clubs from the West of Scotland during World War One, The Dee meet Dundee Hibernian in the first official league derby at Dens and record a 5-1 win in the first game of the 1917/18 season. In front of a restricted war crowd of 4,000, the Dark Blues' goals are scored by Tommy Taylor (2), Sid Lamb, Frank Murray and Jim Heron.

## SATURDAY 18th AUGUST 1979

Ian Redford sets a new club record of scoring four goals in a Scottish League Premier Division match as newly promoted Dundee defeat St Mirren 4-1 at Dens in the first home league game of the season.

## SATURDAY 19th AUGUST 1899

Dundee's new ground Dens Park is officially opened with a friendly against Edinburgh side St Bernards with Chairman Baillie Robertson kicking the match off for the visitors. The prodigal 'Plum' Longair returns and is amongst nine local players to line up for Dundee. One of them, Fred McDiarmid is the historic first goalscorer at the new ground in a 1-1 draw in front of a 10,000 crowd on a beautiful sunny afternoon.

## SATURDAY 19th AUGUST 1995

Neil McCann scores four as Dundee start the League Cup 'Road to Hampden' with a 6-0 second round win over East Stirlingshire. With Shire's Firs Park unable to host the tie, the match is moved to Falkirk's Brockville and further goals from Morten Weighorst and Jim Hamilton see The Dee safely through.

## SATURDAY 19th AUGUST 1989

A Keith Wright hat-trick helps Dundee defeat Dundee United 4-3 at Dens after being 2-0 down after just 24 minutes. Keith Wright pulls the Dark Blues level with a brace just before half time but Mixu Paatelainen makes it 3-2 to The Arabs just after the break. Keith Wright completes his treble on the hour and Joe McBride wins a scintillating derby with a free kick curled over the Tannadice wall and into the top corner 17 minutes from time.

## SATURDAY 20th AUGUST 1960

Dundee begin their 1960 League Cup campaign in devastating form, notching six straight wins in their section and scoring an impressive 23 goals. One of those wins is a 4-1 victory over Aberdeen at Pittodrie thanks to goals from Alan Gilzean (2), Alan Cousin and Andy Penman.

## SATURDAY 21st AUGUST 1965

Dundee start the season in a tough League Cup section alongside Celtic, Dundee United and Motherwell but a Kenny Cameron double gives Dundee a 2-0 win over Celtic at Parkhead.

## WEDNESDAY 22nd AUGUST 1984

Dundee win their first game of the season with a 3-0 League Cup first round victory over Hamilton Academical at Dens thanks to goals from Ray Stephen, Walker McCall and Robert Connor, netting his first goal for The Dee.

## WEDNESDAY 23rd AUGUST 1961

Dundee's title-winning Scottish League Division One campaign starts with a 3-1 win over Falkirk at Brockville. Gordon Smith gets his first league goal for the club against manager Bob Shankly's former club when he nets an Andy Penman cross which Alan Gilzean had dummied. Two Smith crosses set up headed goals for Alan Cousin and Bobby Wishart. With no floodlights on, Wyles scores a consolation goal in the 90th minute past an unsighted Pat Liney in the Dundee goal in the midweek darkness.

## SATURDAY 24th AUGUST 1946

In front of 21,000 at Tannadice, goals from Albert Juliussen and Ronnie Turnbull give Dundee a 2-1 win over Dundee United as they look to retain their Scottish League B Division title and secure promotion in the first official season after World War Two.

## SATURDAY 25th AUGUST 1962

Scottish champions Dundee meet Dundee United at Dens in a League Cup sectional tie and the home crowd chant 'We want Penman' after news that 'The Penalty King' Andy had handed in a transfer request. He withdraws it shortly after the 2-1 win over United, secured thanks to a brace from Penman's right-wing partner, Gordon Smith. 'The Gay Gordon' scores his first past future Dee boss Donald McKay in the United goal when he cuts in from the touchline and fires in with the wind's help from 35 yards.

## SATURDAY 26th AUGUST 1893

Dundee record their first ever win with a 3-2 victory away to Renton at Tontine Park in West Dunbartonshire thanks to goals from Jimmy Dundas and George Reid (2), scoring his first goals for the club.

## SATURDAY 26th AUGUST 1944

With Dundee having returned from a four-year abeyance due to the Second World War in which Dens Park is utilised as a store for the Decontamination (Food) Service, a Ronnie Turnbull brace gives The Dee a 2-1 win over Dundee United in front of 15,500 at Tannadice. It maintains the Dark Blues 100% start to the season under new manager George Anderson.

## SATURDAY 27th AUGUST 1921

Willie Cowan and Johnny Bell goals give Dundee a 2-0 win over Third Lanark in front of 17,000 at Dens Park for their first win of the season after a draw and a defeat in their opening two games.

## SATURDAY 28th AUGUST 1926

Andy Campbell becomes the first player from any side to score a hat-trick in a Dundee derby when he nets four as Dundee defeat Dundee United in front of 20,000 at Dens. His four goals against United are a feat never equalled by any Dundee player in league or cup derbies since and a further strike from Jim Meagher gives The Dee a 5-0 victory. It is their highest ever victory against the Tannadice men who are relegated in bottom place at the end of the season.

## THURSDAY 28th AUGUST 2003

Dundee face KS Vllaznia in the second leg of the Uefa Cup preliminary round. There is one change from the first leg in Albania with Beto Carranza coming in for Garry Brady and within two minutes a brilliant defence-splitting pass by the little Argentinean allows Nacho Novo to fire home. Carranza is then taken off injured but just before half time his replacement, Juan Sara, adds a second. After the break Gavin Rae scores one of the best goals ever seen at Dens Park when he thunders a 22-yarder in off the bar and near the end, Novo gets his second and Dundee's fourth to complete the 6-0 aggregate rout.

## SATURDAY 29th AUGUST 1987

Tommy Coyne equals Ian Redford's record of scoring four goals in a Scottish League Premier Division match and a Keith Wright strike gives Dundee a 5-0 win over Dunfermline Athletic on a lovely sunny afternoon at Dens.

## SATURDAY 30th AUGUST 1924

Dundee secure their first victory of the season when top scorer Dave Halliday nets four and his strike partner Davie McLean two as Dundee defeat Heart of Midlothian 6-0 in front of 17,000 at Dens.

## WEDNESDAY 30th AUGUST 1939

Four days before war is declared and league football is suspended, Dundee enjoy a 6-1 win over Dundee United at Dens in the Forfarshire Cup first round thanks to a hat-trick from Charlie McGillivray, a brace from Archie Coats and a Robertson own goal.

## WEDNESDAY 30th AUGUST 1995

The Dark Blues meet Premier Division Kilmarnock in the third round of the Scottish League Cup and, trailing 1-0 at half time, hit back after the break to secure a fantastic 3-1 win. It is goals from George Shaw, Morten Weighorst and Jim Hamilton which sends First Division Dundee into the quarter-finals for the first time in seven years.

## SATURDAY 31st AUGUST 1929

A Frank Townrow goal gives Dundee their first home win of the season and a 1-0 win over Dundee United in front of 16,000 at Dens.

# DUNDEE FC
## *On This Day*

# SEPTEMBER

## WEDNESDAY 1st SEPTEMBER 1965

Only two points separate Dundee, Dundee United, Celtic and Motherwell in the League Cup section and Dundee cross the road to Tannadice to take on the group leaders. Amidst a tension-ridden atmosphere, two goals by Kenny Cameron either side of half time puts Dundee in the driving seat before Gillespie pulls one back with a penalty on the hour. However, 19 minutes from time, Steve Murray settles the issue when he sends a low shot past Dundee United keeper and future Dee manager Donald Mackay.

## WEDNESDAY 2nd SEPTEMBER 1987

In front of a capacity 19,817 Dens Park crowd, Dundee knock Dundee United out of the quarter-final of the League Cup thanks to the Cobra and the Mongoose. After only six minutes ex-Dee Iain Ferguson heads United in front and, for the next hour, Dundee's goal comes under siege. However, brilliantly marshalled by Jim Duffy, they survive and grow more into the game as it wears on. With just five minutes left ex-Arab Tommy Coyne slides home a Tosh McKinlay cross to level and five minutes into extra time, the home end erupts when Keith Wright finishes off a brilliant move by Coyne and Graham Harvey, who had come on two minutes earlier for Vince Mennie. It sends The Dee into the semis and gains revenge for the Scottish Cup semi defeat at Tynecastle five months before.

## TUESDAY 3rd SEPTEMBER 1996

First Division Dundee knock Premier Division Dundee United out the League Cup on penalties. On a warm, humid evening, 11,839 turn up at Tannadice for the third round tie and see Owen Coyle give United the lead on 20 minutes against the run of play. The Dark Blues battle back to level through a Jim Hamilton penalty and there is no further scoring in the end-to-end game. Seven minutes into extra time Chic Charnley deftly rolls the ball along United's penalty area to Kevin Bain whose shot deflects off Jim Hamilton and into the net but with ten minutes left Gary McSwegan makes it 2-2 to take the tie to penalties. Charnley, Tosh and McKeown score for Dundee with Ray McKinnon and Neil Duffy doing likewise for the home side. Billy Thomson in the Dundee goal then saves from McSwegan before Iain Ferguson, who was sent on by Jim Duffy in the last seconds with a view to taking a penalty, keeps his nerve to score and send The Dee through on a memorable night.

### TUESDAY 4th SEPTEMBER 1979

Dundee travel to Bramall Lane to take on Sheffield United in the second round of the Anglo-Scottish Cup. Bobby Geddes makes his debut for The Dee but can't prevent them losing the first leg 2-1, with Billy Williamson getting the away goal. A week later The Blades come to Dens for the second leg and win 1-0 thanks to a goal from ex-Dee John McPhail to progress 3-1 on aggregate.

### WEDNESDAY 5th SEPTEMBER 1962

Dundee make their European debut and shock the continent with an 8-1 home win over German champions Cologne in the European Cup preliminary round first leg. Hemmersbach heads an Andy Penman cross into his own net on nine minutes to give Dundee the lead and in quick succession Bobby Wishart and Hugh Robertson add two more. Alan Gilzean and Gordon Smith score a further two to give the Dark Blues a 5-0 half-time lead. West German keeper Fritz Ewart doesn't appear for the second half after failing to recover from a second minute collision with Alan Cousin. Right-back Regh takes over in goal and a header from Penman and two more from Gilzean to complete his hat-trick give Dundee an 8-0 lead before the ball bounces off Alex Hamilton for a Cologne consolation goal. It is one of Dundee's best ever displays and arguably their greatest ever result.

### THURSDAY 6th SEPTEMBER 1945

Doug Cowie signs from Junior side Aberdeen St Clements and would become one of the greatest ever Dees making a club record 446 appearances. He plays in two World Cups with Scotland as a Dundee player, wins 20 full caps and would win the Scottish League Cup in 1951 and 1952. The player with 'the touch of an angel' is inducted into the inaugural Dundee Hall of Fame in 2009 and has a lounge named after him at Dens.

## SATURDAY 6th SEPTEMBER 1947

Dundee's 1947/48 season kicks off with a League Cup section that includes 'A' Division sides Rangers, Celtic and Third Lanark and in the Celtic game at Dens goals from Johnny Pattillo, Ernie Ewen (2) and Albert Juliussen give the newly promoted side a 4-1 win. At the end of the match violent scenes erupt on the terracing with widespread bottle throwing by disgruntled Celtic fans.

## SATURDAY 7th SEPTEMBER 1963

Dundee record their first league win of the season with a 4-2 win over Aberdeen at Pittodrie thanks to goals from Alan Gilzean (2), Kenny Cameron and Andy Penman.

## SATURDAY 8th SEPTEMBER 1984

Archie Knox's summer signings finally come good when Dundee beat Dundee United 4-3 at Tannadice. The key to the success is in midfield where the speedy Stuart Rafferty is complemented by the craft of Robert Connor and the tackling of John Brown. Three times Dundee take the lead through Derek McWilliams, Tosh McKinlay (with a superb volley) and Colin Harris, only for United to level, but with 14 minutes remaining John Brown powers a header past Billy Thomson for the winner.

## SATURDAY 9th SEPTEMBER 1961

In Dundee's first home league game of their title winning season, the Dark Blues maintain their record of never having lost to Dundee United at Dens as they beat their neighbours 4-1 in front of a crowd of 20,000. Dundee rip holes in the United defence with their short passing game and pacy attack and Andy Penman opens the scoring with his third goal in four derbies. Gordon Smith scores his first goal at Dens before United captain Jimmy Briggs puts past his own keeper. Gillespie pulls one back for the visitors before Hugh Robertson adds a fourth before the end to give The Dee their biggest win over United since 1926.

## SATURDAY 10th SEPTEMBER 1938

Dundee draw 2-2 in the Scottish League Division Two at Dens with the original Edinburgh City (founded in 1928 and disbanded in

1955 before being reformed in 1986). The Dee's goals are scored by Archie Coats and Harry Sneddon.

## SATURDAY 11th SEPTEMBER 1971

Dundee defeat Dundee United 6-4 in an amazing derby at Dens to give The Dee their first league success at home over their neighbours since 1961. A brace each from Alex Bryce, Gordon Wallace and Jocky Scott earns the famous win but it could have been a rout had the Dark Blues not taken their foot off the gas. After scoring the sixth with 20 minutes left, they allow The Arabs to pull two goals back for a flattering scoreline.

## WEDNESDAY 12th SEPTEMBER 1956

The legend of Johnnie Scobie is born as Dundee defeat Division Two Dundee United 7-3 at a rainswept Dens in the League Cup quarter-final. Pacy right-winger Jimmy Chalmers gives United a torrid time and is the hero with a hat-trick. The Dark Blues' other goals are scored by Gordon Black, George Christie, George O'Hara and George Merchant. The game is immortalised by Dundee fans in the reworking of the traditional Scottish song *'We're No Awa to Bide Awa'* which starts with 'As I was walking doon the Overgate, I met wee Johnnie Scobie' and finishes with, 'And when we got there, the terracing was bare but we gave United seven!'

## SATURDAY 12th SEPTEMBER 1964

Dundee defeat Dundee United 4-1 at Tannadice as a Dundee legend starts to makes his name. Lewis Thom puts Jerry Kerr's United ahead on 28 minutes but seven minutes later Alan Cousin equalises with a well judged lob. Soon after the break the in-form Bobby Waddell makes it 2-1 before a late double by 16-year-old John 'Jocky' Scott completes a famous derby success.

## WEDNESDAY 13th SEPTEMBER 1972

Dundee defeat Norwich City at 2-1 Dens in the first round of the Texaco Cup thanks to goals from Iain Scott and Duncan Lambie. However, a 2-0 defeat at Carrow Road in the second leg a fortnight later sends The Canaries through 3-2 on aggregate.

## SATURDAY 13th SEPTEMBER 2014

Defender Thomas Konrad scores his first goal for the club in a 1-0 win over St Johnstone at McDiarmid Park, Perth in the Scottish Premiership. The German centre-half had joined the club in the summer and would stay for two seasons, making 69 appearances. Konrad's only other goal for The Dee was in a famous Scottish Cup win against Aberdeen two months later. After opening the scoring in four minutes, 'Tam' puts through his own net before half-time but an injury time winner from David Clarkson sees The Dee through to the fifth round.

## SATURDAY 14th SEPTEMBER 1895

Dundee defeat Third Lanark 4-3 at the original Cathkin Park (Thirds played at the original Cathkin Park from their foundation in 1872 until 1903 when they took over Queen's Park's Hampden Park ground, renaming it New Cathkin Park, whilst Queen's Park moved to a new Hampden Park in Mount Florida) thanks to a hat-trick from Willie Lonie and a strike from Bill Hendry. Dundee would finish the season fifth, one point ahead of 'The Hi-His'.

## WEDNESDAY 15th SEPTEMBER 1971

A 'new look' Dundee, wearing white shirts and dark blue shorts for season 1971/72, meet Akademisk Boldklub of Copenhagen in the revamped Uefa Cup at Dens. A first-leg crowd of 9,000 witness goals from Alex Bryce (2), Gordon Wallace and Duncan Lambie to give The Dee a 4-2 lead to take to Denmark.

## SATURDAY 16th SEPTEMBER 1911

Dundee defeat Celtic 3-1 in front of 20,000 at Dens with a brace from Jimmy Bellamy and a goal from Sandy MacFarlane. MacFarlane would later manage The Dee for two spells in the Roaring Twenties and the 1910 Scottish Cup winner is inducted into the club's Hall of Fame in 2015 with a Heritage Award. The award is received on his behalf by DFC Chairman Bill Colvin from author and club historian Kenny Ross.

## SATURDAY 17th SEPTEMBER 1966

In the third derby of the season Dundee 'cross the Great Divide' again to Tannadice where they had lost 2-0 to Dundee United in a League Cup sectional tie and after a 1-1 draw at Dens in the return, avenge that defeat in the league with a 4-1 win thanks to goals from Kenny Cameron, Andy Penman (2) and Derek McKay.

## TUESDAY 17th SEPTEMBER 1996

After losing out to Aberdeen in the League Cup final the year before, a last minute goal from Jim Hamilton knocks the holders out 2-1 at Dens. In a fiercely fought encounter, there are nine bookings and, just before the break, Dundee take the lead when Paul Tosh volleys home from 16 yards. Ex-Dee Billy Dodds makes it 1-1 from the spot before Dean Windass is sent off minutes later for a wild challenge on Chic Charley. With the extra man advantage, Aberdonian Hamilton squirms his half hit effort under Nicky Walker for a last-gasp winner.

## WEDNESDAY 18th SEPTEMBER 1968

Hat-tricks from Jocky Scott and George McLean give Dundee a 6-0 League Cup quarter-final, second leg win over Stranraer at Dens. A 4-0 win at Stair Park the previous week sees The Dee through to the semis 10-0 on aggregate.

## WEDNESDAY 18th SEPTEMBER 1974

In the first round of the Uefa Cup Dundee travel to Belgium to face RWD Molenbeek and a solid defensive display in the Brussels suburb leaves The Dee with a far from insurmountable 1-0 deficit for the home leg.

## WEDNESDAY 19th SEPTEMBER 1973

Dundee lose their unbeaten home record in Europe when they lose 3-1 to Twente Enschede in the first round of the Uefa Cup. After 30 minutes Thomson Allan races 40 yards from his goal only to be lobbed from the halfway line. After the break George Stewart equalises with a header but almost immediately the Dutch side regain the lead and score a third towards the end.

## SATURDAY 19th SEPTEMBER 1992

In the first derby for three years, a Billy Dodds penalty gives Dundee a 1-0 win over Dundee United at Tannadice. The Dark Blues are under pressure for most of the game until Ivo Den Bieman is sent crashing in the box with just ten minutes left. The game will be remembered for United's Argentinean forward Victor Ferreyra spitting at Jim Duffy at full time and throwing a punch in his direction for which he is retrospectively red carded and then allowed to return home.

## SATURDAY 19th SEPTEMBER 1998

Dariusz Adamzuck scores an injury-time equaliser as Dundee come back from 2-0 down against Dundee United at Dens. McSwegan and Olofsson had United ahead with just 20 minutes left but Eddie Annand pulls one back almost immediately with a fine header. As the game moves into injury time Iain Anderson's left wing cross is headed back by Willie Falconer and met by the inrushing Pole who heads powerfully for goal. Sieb Dykstra gets a hand to it but can't prevent it spinning into the net to spark an invasion on to the track by Dundee fans. New Dundee United manager Paul Sturrock says on *Sportscene* at night that, 'it felt like a defeat.'

## WEDNESDAY 20th SEPTEMBER 1995

In one of the greatest games ever seen at Dens, First Division Dundee knock top flight Heart of Midlothian out of the League Cup quarter-final on penalties after a thrilling 4-4 draw. A George Shaw double gives the Dark Blues a well merited 2-0 lead before Colquhoun and McPherson make it 2-2 with 17 minutes left. Shaw then pressurises Hearts keeper Henry Smith into kicking across his box to Paul Tosh who crashes the ball home, but ex-Dee Alan Lawrence levels right on full time. In extra time Morten Weighorst brilliantly shimmies past a couple of defenders before firing a dipping 25-yard shot into the net before a John Robertson spot kick takes it to penalties. Hearts keeper Smith and ex-Dee Willie Jamieson miss their kicks allowing man of the match Weighorst to roll home his kick and send The Dee into the semis 5-4 on pens.

## WEDNESDAY 20th SEPTEMBER 2000

The night of the 'Juan-Two-Three' as a Juan Sara hat-trick gives Dundee a 3-0 win over Dundee United on a famous night at Dens. Sara is aided by a majestic performance by Giorgi Nemsadze in midfield and a dazzling wing display by Javier Artero, but the match will likely be remembered as much for the horrendous double tackle on Fabian Cabellero by Jason De Vos and Kevin McDonald which puts the Argentinean out the game for six months.

## SATURDAY 21st SEPTEMBER 1985

With recent signing Jim Duffy a defensive rock, Stuart Rafferty scores a spectacular long-range drive to give The Dee a 1-0 win over Rangers at Ibrox. It is Dundee's third win in Govan in the calendar year.

## FRIDAY 22nd SEPTEMBER 1950

Dundee sign Scottish international superstar Billy Steel for a world-record fee of £23,500 from Derby County. The inside-right would score 45 goals in 131 appearances and would help Dundee to back-to-back League Cup wins in 1951 and 1952. 'Budgem' is inducted into the inaugural DFC Hall of Fame in 2009 with a Legends Award after being voted in by the fans.

## SATURDAY 23rd SEPTEMBER 1961

Despite the convention at this time being for the home side to change shirts to avoid any clash, it is The Dee who change and wear white shirts at Tynecastle against Hearts. A short back pass from Jambos' captain John Cumming is intercepted by Andy Penman who squares to Alan Gilzean for a tap-in. Gillie gets his second double of the title-winning season when he heads home a Hugh Robertson cross to secure a 2-0 win.

## SATURDAY 24th SEPTEMBER 1988

Tommy Coyne scores his first goal of the season to give Dave Smith's Dundee a 1-0 win over reigning champions Celtic at Dens who have Alan Rough in the goal. The goal goes in off 'The Cobra's' shin after a great run and cross down the left from Keith Wright and after scoring 37 times the previous campaign, it is TC's first goal of the season.

## THURSDAY 24th SEPTEMBER 2003

Dundee faced Serie A side AC Perugia in the Uefa Cup first round after the Italians qualifed by winning the InterToto Cup. New signings Craig Burley and Fabrizio Ravanelli are paraded at half time but, five minutes later, Di Loretto gave the Italians the lead. Lee Wilkie and Nacho Novo then both claimed the equaliser on 63 minutes with Novo stating he got the last touch on Wilkie's header, but Perugia leave with a 2-1 first leg lead when Fusani hooked home a late winner.

## SATURDAY 25th SEPTEMBER 1915

Top scorer Davie Brown scores five and Alec Troup two as Dundee defeat Queen's Park 7-1 at Dens in an official wartime Division One fixture. Troup had recently been persuaded to sign by a Dundee director while he is working up a ladder repairing a roof for an undertaker and when he comes down to sign a contract, he does so by putting pen to paper on top of a new coffin. It is a macabre start to his Dundee career but he would go on to become a Dundee legend and is inducted into the club's Hall of Fame in 2017 with a Heritage Award, accepted on his behalf by grandson Brian Taylor.

## WEDNESDAY 26th SEPTEMBER 1962

Dubbed 'The Battle of Cologne' Dundee survived a brutal Cologne onslaught to progress 8-5 on aggregate in the European Cup preliminary round, having gone to West Germany with an 8-1 lead. On seven minutes Alex Hamilton palmed a Schaefer header over the bar and Habig nets the penalty. Dundee went down to ten men when keeper Bert Slater was stretchered off on 27 minutes after being kicked in the head saving from Mueller. Mueller then scores past stand-in Andy Penman before Schaefer gave Cologne a 3-0 half-time lead. Ian Ure scores an own goal shortly after the break but Dundee were restored to a full complement when a heavily bandaged Slater returned on the wing and then went back in goal to watch Habig hit another penalty, this time against the bar. Dundee saw the game out against severe intimidation both on and off the park.

## WEDNESDAY 27th SEPTEMBER 1967

In Amsterdam's Olympic Stadium Dundee met DWS Amsterdam in the Inter-Cities Fairs Cup first round under floodlights of dubious quality. John Arrol makes a great penalty save and George McLean scores but it can't prevent the Dark Blues losing the first leg 2-1.

## SATURDAY 28th SEPTEMBER 2013

Craig Beattie scores his first goal for Dundee after a brace from Peter MacDonald cancels out Greenock Morton's opener in a 3-1 win at Dens. Beattie and MacDonald's goals are crucial on the way to winning the SPFL Championship and promotion back to the top flight at the first attempt.

## WEDNESDAY 29th SEPTEMBER 1971

Dundee travelled to Copenhagen for a Uefa Cup first round second leg match with Akademisk Boldklub. The Danes posed few problems in the second leg and, shortly after half time, John Duncan scored the only goal with a header to give The Dee a 5-2 aggregate win.

## SATURDAY 30th SEPTEMBER 1961

Dundee record their first win in three matches against George Young's Third Lanark having drawn 1-1 twice in the League Cup sectional ties at the start of the season. Dundee show their title winning potential with a comfortable 3-1 win thanks to two headed Alan Gilzean goals from Bobby Seith crosses and an Alan Cousin strike from the corner of the box.

# DUNDEE FC
## *On This Day*

# OCTOBER

## SATURDAY 1st OCTOBER 1898

Dundee recorded their biggest win of the season when they defeat Partick Thistle 5-1 at Carolina Port with goals from James McLay, Stuart Methven (2), John Bunce and Jim Gerrard.

## WEDNESDAY 2nd OCTOBER 1974

RWD Molenbeek come to Dens for a Uefa Cup first round second leg tie with nine internationalists in their side. John Duncan levels the aggregate score with a 12th minute header before Tuegals and Beskamp give the classy Belgians a 2-1 lead on the night. Jocky Scott pulls one back before two goals by Wellens in the last 20 minutes gives Racing White a 5-2 aggregate win.

## SATURDAY 2nd OCTOBER 2010

With a second administration on the horizon the players go into a pre-match huddle for the first time before they defeat Greenock Morton 2-1 at Dens thanks to a Matt Lockwood penalty and a Colin McMenamin goal. The win is the first of the club record 23-game unbeaten league run.

## WEDNESDAY 3rd OCTOBER 1973

Dundee travelled to the Netherlands and lose 4-2 to Twente Enschede in the Uefa Cup first round, second leg to bow out 7-3 on aggregate. Dave Johnson and Iain Scott, who were Dundee's substitutes in the League Cup final in December, scored Dundee's consolation goals.

## TUESDAY 3rd OCTOBER 2000

Dundee shocked the footballing world by signing Argentine superstar Claudio Caniggia. He would make a huge impression in his one season at Dens, being nominated for the SPFA Player of the Year and winning the Andrew De Vries Memorial Trophy for Dundee Player of the Year. He states when he signs that he wants to get back into the Argentina squad for the World Cup in 2002 and achieves his aim when called up for the tournament in Japan and South Korea.

THE PRE MATCH HUDDLE BECAME A SYMBOL OF THE DEE-FIANT SPIRIT THAT SAVED THE CLUB DURING THE SECOND ADMINISTRATION

## SATURDAY 4th OCTOBER 1952

Dundee defeat reigning League champions Hibernian 2-1 in front of 44,200 at Tynecastle in the League Cup semi-final to reach their second successive final. Lawrie Reilly gives Hibs a 1-0 half-time lead but seven minutes into the second half Billy Steel levels for The Dee. With manager George Anderson ill and listening on the wireless in a nursing home in Aberdeen, he hears Bobby Flavell grab the winner with ten minutes left.

## WEDNESDAY 4th OCTOBER 1967

In the Inter-Cities Fairs Cup first round, second leg against DWS Amsterdam, Sammy Wilson delights the 15,000 crowd when, in just four minutes, he fires the ball past Schriijvers to make it 2-2 on aggregate. On the hour Jim McLean scores a penalty before heading his second near the end for a 3-0 win to send the Dark Blues through 4-2 on aggregate.

## SATURDAY 5th OCTOBER 1895

Dundee defeat Edinburgh side St Bernards 4-1 at Carolina Port with goals from Harry Vail, Jimmy Dundas (pen), Dave McDonald and Bill Sawers. McDonald would finish the 1895/96 season as top goalscorer with just six goals.

## SATURDAY 6th OCTOBER 1956

Dundee drew 0-0 with Partick Thistle at Ibrox in the League Cup semi-final. In the replay at the same venue three days later Thistle raced into a 2-0 lead before George Christie and George O'Hara made it 2-2 at the interval. Dundee dominated the second half but were hit with a sucker punch when Davidson hits a free kick past Bill Brown with 20 minutes left to progress to the final.

## SATURDAY 7th OCTOBER 1961

With Rangers inactive due to international commitments, Dundee move to the top of the league for the first time in their championship-winning season with a 5-3 home win over Kilmarnock. It's a sweet day for Andy Penman as he scores a hat-trick against the side he broke his leg against the previous year. Alan Gilzean is also on target and the scoring is rounded off in the 87th minute when Killie full-back Matt Watson heads past his own keeper.

## WEDNESDAY 8th OCTOBER 1980

First Division Dundee face reigning Premier Division champions Aberdeen in the League Cup quarter-final first leg at Dens and are unlucky not to win against Alex Ferguson's side. Despite enjoying long spells of pressure, the Dark Blues have to be content with a commendable 0-0 draw to take up north for the second leg.

## WEDNESDAY 9th OCTOBER 1968

In new manager John Prentice's second match in charge, Dundee faced Bob Shankly's Hibernian in a League Cup semi-final at Tynecastle. Prentice was recommended by previous boss Bobby Ancell, who had taken over from Shankly as he felt a younger man should be at the helm and stood down to become youth coach. George McLean puts the Dark Blues in front after six minutes but 30 seconds later Colin Stein equalises. The Dee are denied a second successive League Cup final appearance when Alan McGraw scores the winner with 16 minutes left.

## SATURDAY 10th OCTOBER 1959

There is no glory start for Bob Shankly when a 3-1 home defeat by league leaders Rangers in his first game leaves the Dark Blues near the foot of the table. Hugh Robertson scores the first goal of the Dark Blue Shankly era.

## SATURDAY 10th OCTOBER 1970

A John Duncan goal is enough to give Dundee a 1-0 win over Ayr United at Somerset Park. Like his boyhood hero Alan Gilzean, Duncan is also strong in the air and soon gains the nickname 'Gillie' but more unusually he prefers to wear rugby boots which he claims give him a more powerful shot. Duncan would score 109 goals in 188 appearances and is inducted into the club's Hall of Fame in 2015 with a Legends Award.

## WEDNESDAY 11th OCTOBER 1967

Dundee reached their first League Cup Final in 15 years when they defeat St Johnstone 3-1 at Tannadice in the semi-final. Gordon Whitelaw heads the Saints into the lead just before the interval but after the break defender George Millar is twice pressurised into putting the ball his own net to give the Dark Blues the lead. Billy Campbell is then upended by Benny Rooney in the box on 72 minutes and Jim McLean steps up to score from the spot and send The Dee to Hampden.

## SATURDAY 12th OCTOBER 1957

Championship-winning goalkeeper Pat Liney signs for Dundee from Dalry Thistle. Liney would make 126 appearances for The Dee and is a pivotal player in the title win when he makes a crucial penalty save in the penultimate match in April 1962. Pat is inducted into Dundee's Hall of Fame with a Legends Award in 2011 and is named Honorary President of the club later the same year.

## SATURDAY 13th OCTOBER 1951

Dundee meet Motherwell in the League Cup semi-final at Ibrox. *The Sunday Post* refers to the game as 'an all time classic' but it is unlikely anyone in claret and amber would agree as Dundee run out 5-1 winners. It has all the thrills of a knockout battle, performed as *The Sporting Post* put it 'in masterly style' and for Dundee, their movement is 'silky and intelligent and a joy to watch'. The game is much tighter than the score suggests when, after leading 2-1 in a thrilling first half thanks to goals from George Christie and Bobby Flavell, the second period sees the Dark Blues come under intense pressure as Motherwell seek to draw level. However, with 19 minutes remaining Johnny Pattillo grabs a third before Flavell adds another two near the end to give The Dee a rather flattering 5-1 scoreline to send them to Hampden.

## SATURDAY 14th OCTOBER 1961

Dundee win 4-2 at Motherwell with goals from Andy Penman (pen), Alan Cousin, Gordon Smith and Alan Gilzean. With the release of Doug Cowie in the summer, Penman has taken over the spot kick duties and the opener is his first league penalty for The Dee. Manager Bob Shankly describes the win as 'The best performance of the League winning season' at the end of the campaign.

## SATURDAY 14th OCTOBER 2000

Dundee travel to Pittodrie and, disappointingly for the large travelling support, new signing Claudio Caniggia starts on the bench as he is somewhat short of match practice. Player-manager Ivano Bonetti opens the scoring with a delightful 25-yard chip over Ryan Esson for his first goal for The Dee which he would describe in the post match press conference as 'The best goal that no one will ever remember.' There is near hysteria just before the break when Caniggia comes on to replace Stevie Milne and although Gavin Rae's sending off for retaliation on Phil Maguire makes things harder, 'The Bird' sets the seal on a memorable afternoon when he races on to a perfectly weighted Giorgi Nemsadze pass to slide the ball inside the far post in the dying seconds. The match is also a farewell to Dundee goalkeeper Robert Douglas who joins Celtic two days later for a club record fee received of £1.2 million.

## SATURDAY 15th OCTOBER 1983

A double from Iain Ferguson and a goal from Walker McCall gives Dundee a 3-2 home win over Rangers. Ferguson would finish the season as top goalscorer for the third campaign in a row with 20 and in the summer would move to Ibrox for a fee of £200,000 after scoring eight goals against the Light Blues.

## WEDNESDAY 15th OCTOBER 2003

Dundee travel to Italy for the Uefa Cup first round second leg tie with AC Perugia and 2,500 Dees make the journey to lend their support. On a bitterly cold night at the Renato Curi Stadium, the Umbrians dominate the first half with Julian Speroni making a splendid save from English striker Jay Boothroyd to keep Dundee in the tie. The Dark Blues improve after the break with Gavin Rae, Nacho Novo and Lee Wilkie all coming close but with 19 minutes remaining, Perugia substitute Massimo Margiotta scores from close range to make it 1-0 on the night and send the Serie A side through 3-1 on aggregate. It has, however, been a trip to remember with a carnival atmosphere in the university town in the days leading up to the game.

## FRIDAY 15th OCTOBER 2010

Dundee Football Club formally enter administration for the second time in seven years with debts of around £2m and Bryan Jackson and Ann Buchanan of PKF Accountants and Business Advisors take control of the club as joint administrators. As expected, their first task is to reduce the wage costs and they release a number of staff with immediate effect. From the playing staff Mikael Antoine-Curier, Scott Fox, Charlie Grant, Brian Kerr, Njazi Kuqi, Paul McHale, Colin McMenamin, Eric Paton and Dominic Shimmin are released alongside manager Gordon Chisholm, assistant manager Billy Dodds, youth development coach John Holt and ticket office manager-kit man Neil Cosgrove. Under-19 coach Barry Smith is asked to take the manager's job on an interim basis and he is to be assisted by players Robert Douglas and Matt Lockwood. The job of saving the club begins.

### SATURDAY 16th OCTOBER 2010

Amidst all the chaos and conjecture, Dundee actually have a game to play at Stirling Albion 24 hours after going into administration. New boss Barry Smith has the job of lifting the 13 senior players who were left on the books. Astonishingly, after such a week of turmoil and despair, a match would have understandably been the last thing on the mind of the players, but they turn in an excellent performance which trumps anything of recent weeks. In front of a noisy 1,000 strong away support, Dundee dominated the first half before Leigh Griffiths gives The Dee the lead not long after the break. Stirling however, bounce back and equalise despite being down to ten men and although it is one way traffic towards The Binos' goal, Dundee can't grab the winner as every player gives their all.

### SATURDAY 17th OCTOBER 1931

Dundee defeat Celtic 2-0 at Dens in front of a crowd of 18,000, The Dee's largest home attendance of the season. Centre-forward Jim Craigie is the hero, netting a brace which are the last he would score in a Dundee shirt in a short Dark Blue career of seven goals in 12 appearances.

### SATURDAY 18th OCTOBER 1975

Dundee came from behind to beat Dundee United 2-1 at Tannadice in the first ever Premier Division derby. Leading marksman Gordon Wallace gets the equaliser and a Wilson Hoggan penalty wins the game in front of 11,327. Wallace finishes the season as top scorer with 14 goals but would join Dundee United the following season after a spell with Seattle Sounders in the North American Soccer League in the summer.

### TUESDAY 18th OCTOBER 1994

Injuries, suspensions and loss of form allow Kevin Bain to re-establish himself in the side and, along with player-manager Jim Duffy, is outstanding in a floodlit Scottish League Challenge Cup semi-final thriller against Dunfermline at East End Park. Bain, who had captained Scotland to the Under-16 World Cup final in 1989, gives Dundee the lead through a penalty before Neil McCann nets the winner to send The Dee to their second Challenge Cup final with a 2-1 win.

## SATURDAY 19th OCTOBER 2013

Craig Beattie comes off the bench and scores a last minute winner to give Dundee a 2-1 win over Queen of the South at Dens on the way to winning the SPFL Championship. Peter MacDonald gives Dundee a 78th minute lead only for ex-Dee Derek Lyle to level two minutes later before Beattie nets his third goal in four games to seal the win.

## WEDNESDAY 20th OCTOBER 1971

In the second round of the Uefa Cup, Dundee are paired with old European Cup foes Cologne and travel to West Germany for the first leg. Ally Donaldson is recalled in goal and in the first half Duncan Lambie has a goal disallowed for pushing an opponent. After the break Cologne take a controversial lead when Rupp's short corner is dummied by Flohe, only for Rupp to take an illegal second consecutive touch and set up Sheermann to score. Alex Kinninmonth equalises on 75 minutes but Lohr gets a winner for Cologne seven minutes from time.

## SATURDAY 20th OCTOBER 1979

Dundee get revenge for a derby defeat in the opening game of the season when an Eric Sinclair goal gives them a 1-0 win over Dundee United in front of 16,300 at Dens.

## WEDNESDAY 21st OCTOBER 1953

Having played the South African national side three times on their summer tour of the Dominion, they meet again at Dens Park when South Africa embark on a two-month tour of the British Isles and Europe. The match ends in a 3-1 Dundee win thanks to a brace from Albert Henderson and a goal from Gerry Burrell.

## SATURDAY 21st OCTOBER 1961

Dundee travelled to Fife to meet Jock Stein's Dunfermline Athletic at East End Park in their title-winning season and are effectively playing with ten men in these pre-substitute days when Gordon Smith is injured in the first minute. Mailer gives The Pars the lead from the spot after Alex Hamilton had fouled Melrose on 25 minutes but two second half goals from Alan Cousin gives The Dee the points to keep them at the top of the league.

## SATURDAY 22nd OCTOBER 2011

Dundee end a run of four games without a win and moved off the foot of the Scottish League First Division with a comfortable 3-1 win at Somerset Park. The visitors take the lead after 15 minutes when Stephen O'Donnell produces a pin-point cross for Rhys Weston to head home. Matt Lockwood then has a chance to extend their lead after Weston is bundled over in the area, but his weak penalty is saved by Kevin Cuthbert. Leighton Mcintosh does get the second 20 minutes from time with a neat finish. Mark Roberts pulls one back from the penalty spot in the 83rd minute following Lockwood's rash challenge on Moffat, but Steven Milne's fifth goal of the season three minutes later ensures that Ayr United go bottom.

## WEDNESDAY 23rd OCTOBER 1996

Uncharacteristic defensive lapses cost the white-shirted Dee dear in the League Cup semi-final with Heart of Midlothian at Easter Road. Firstly, Billy Thomson fails to control a Dariusz Adamczuk back pass, allowing Beckford to nip in and score at the second attempt before Colin Cameron makes it 2-0 from the spot after Adamczuk's clumsy tackle on Callaghan. Stéphane Paille makes it three on the hour before Jim Hamilton scores a consolation on 73 minutes but the 3-1 defeat means no consecutive League Cup final appearances for Dundee.

## WEDNESDAY 24th OCTOBER 1962

Dundee travel to Lisbon to take on Sporting Clube de Portugal in the European Cup first round first leg. The kick-off is delayed five minutes to allow photographs to be taken of the captains exchanging pennants and in six minutes Alan Gilzean has a chance to open the

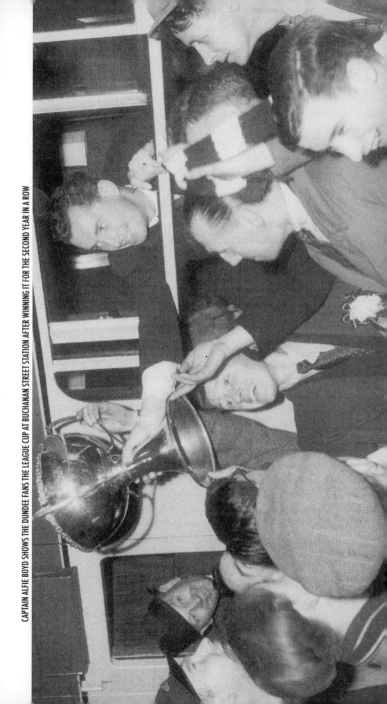

CAPTAIN ALFIE BOYD SHOWS THE DUNDEE FANS THE LEAGUE CUP AT BUCHANAN STREET STATION AFTER WINNING IT FOR THE SECOND YEAR IN A ROW

scoring but overruns the ball when through on goal. After an end
-to-end, evenly matched game, it is Sporting who grab the winner in
the final minute. Bert Slater punches a high cross to Geo who shoots
towards the near post and although Slater recovers to tip it on to
the bar before Bobby Wishart clears off the line, the referee signals
a goal. In celebration the Portuguese crowd throw soft cushions
into the air and they cascade on to the pitch. After the nightmare
in Cologne, Dundee's faith is restored in European football with the
match being described by Tommy Gallacher in *The Courier* as 'One
of the fastest, most gruelling but sportiest European Cup ties ever
seen.'

## SATURDAY 25th OCTOBER 1952

Dundee become the first club to win back-to-back League Cups
when they defeat Kilmarnock 2-0 at a wet and windy Hampden.
Manager George Anderson is ill with pleurisy and listening at home
in Aberdeen to Dundee's third cup final in 12 months on the wireless.
The B Division side from Ayrshire start the brighter and dominate
for large spells but the turning point comes with just ten minutes left
when Jimmy Toner goes to his skipper Alfie Boyd and asks him if
he could switch inside and swap places with Bert Henderson. Cowie
agrees and two minutes later Toner gets the ball from a midfield
mix-up, feints to make out to Henderson on the touchline and with
the Killie defence on the wrong foot, puts a peach of a pass through
to Bobby Flavell. It is the first effective Dundee pass of the game and
the first chance that Flavell has and he shows his appreciation by
firing low past Niven to give Dundee a scarcely deserved lead. Three
minutes from the end the Dark Blues double their lead and make
certain that the cup is coming to Dens for the second year in a row.
Bobby Henderson's long punt reaches the Killie penalty box and as
centre-half Thyne hesitates, Flavell rushes in, the wee centre lets the
ball bounce twice before racing in to thump the ball into the corner
of the net in exactly the same spot as five minutes before.

## WEDNESDAY 25th OCTOBER 1995

'It's a flash of genius from the Dundee youngster which looks like
earning his team a cup final place,' proclaims BBC commentator
Jock Brown after Neil McCann scores a sensational goal against

Airdrieonians in the last few minutes in the League Cup semi-final at McDiarmid Park. With so much at stake on a windy night, the Dark Blues enjoy over three quarters of the crowd and they start well with a number of chances, eventually breaking the deadlock just before the interval when Paul Tosh rams home a Tommy McQueen cross. With only seven minutes left Dundee receive a stunning blow when Paul Duffield stoops to head home the equaliser. Five minutes later, George Shaw sends the ball wide to McCann and the winger speeds the ball into the box with everyone expecting a cross. However, he lobs the ball over John Martin's head before it dips into the net off the inside of the far post and after a moment's hesitation, the Dundee fans go wild as they realise what McCann has just done with his audacious effort. Dundee win 2-1 and book their place in their first final for 15 years and it means much more than that as on the eve of the match, manager Jim Duffy has been privately told that they simply have to reach the final to survive due to the club's financial plight.

## SATURDAY 26th OCTOBER 1896

A visit to Celtic Park ends in an 11-0 rout, a club record defeat that still stands, although Dundee were severely handicapped by being down to nine men in these pre-substitute days. Captain 'Plum' Longair has to go off late in the first half and then left-back Frank Ferrier is also unable to resume after the break in what is his only appearance for The Dee.

## SATURDAY 27th OCTOBER 1951

Dundee defeat Rangers 3-2 in front of 92,325 at Hampden to win the League Cup and their first major trophy in 41 years. After a bright start from the white-shirted Dee, Willie Findlay puts Rangers ahead on 21 minutes against the run of play. Dundee draw level two minutes into the second half when the ever-alert Bobby Flavell fires George Christie's cross into the net. On 69 minutes, Jack Cowan clears the ball from the box and the ball goes to Flavell, who passes it on with a dainty flick. Johnny Pattillo comes steaming in and he hits Bobby's pass on the run, a beauty which flies into the Rangers' net to give The Dee a 2-1 lead. With two minutes left Rangers draw level in controversial circumstances. George Young takes a free kick just inside the Dundee half and floats it into the Dark Blues' box and when Bill Brown goes up to catch it, he is nudged by Willie Thornton and the ball floats into the net. From the restart, however, Billy Steel is fouled just inside the Rangers' half and Dundee have one last chance to grab a winner. With just 30 seconds remaining, Steel places the ball on the ground, preparing to take the kick and, as he does so, Alfie Boyd speeds past him saying, 'I'm going to the right of the goal so try to chip the ball over to me.' Steel replies, 'I'll place it on your head, Alfie,' as he is teeing up the ball and when he takes the free kick, he does exactly that, dropping it to the captain eight yards out. Boyd leaps up, closes his eyes and heads it for all it is worth and when he opens his eyes the ball is in the back of the net and Dundee have won the League Cup for the first time.

## SATURDAY 27th OCTOBER 2001

Temuri Ketsbaia and Massimo Beghetto make their debuts against Hibernian at Easter Road but it is two young Scots who take centre stage. Gavin Rae, the Scottish Premier League Player of the Month for October, runs half the length of the field to score and although Hibs level, Steven Milne, the club record holder for most substitute appearances, comes off the bench to net a last-minute winner.

## SATURDAY 28th OCTOBER 1967

In one of the best finals ever seen at the National Stadium Dundee lose 5-3 to Celtic in the League Cup. On a bright, sunny day, 10,000 Dees are in the 66,000 crowd but they see their side go 2-0 down after ten minutes before George McLean pulls one back on 25 minutes. A frenetic second half sees Stevie Chalmers make it 3-1 with 17 minutes left before Jim McLean scores from close range from a corner. Bobby Lennox pounces on a defensive mix-up to make it 4-2 but George McLean reduces the deficit five minutes from time. As the whole Dundee team charge forward in search of an equaliser, Willie Wallace breaks away to make the final score 5-3 and secure the League Cup for the reigning European Cup champions.

## WEDNESDAY 29th OCTOBER 1980

In mid-September Dundee pay a club record fee of £61,000 for Cammy Fraser from Hearts and he is the hero as Dundee cause a huge shock in the League Cup quarter-final second leg. Dundee travel to Pittodrie to face Scottish champions Aberdeen and Fraser crashes home the winner from 15 yards with five minutes left for a 1-0 aggregate win.

## SATURDAY 29th OCTOBER 1988

Since the arrival of Tommy Coyne and Keith Wright, Graham Harvey has spent a lot of time on the bench but manager Dave Smith starts him at Celtic Park and he plays a huge part in coming back from 2-0 down to win 3-2. After laying one on for Stevie Frail, Harvey brilliantly beats two defenders to equalise and, just before half-time, his netbound header is rammed home by Stuart Rafferty for the second win over Celtic that season.

## WEDNESDAY 29th OCTOBER 2003

Fabrizio Ravanelli comes off the bench and scores a seven minute hat-trick in the League Cup against Clyde at Broadwood. It's the 'White Feather's' first goals for The Dee and they progress 5-3 to the quarter-final with Nacho Novo and Lee Wilkie getting the other goals.

## SATURDAY 30th OCTOBER 1920

Jimmy Bell sets a new club record which, to date, still stands when he scores for a ninth consecutive game in a 3-1 win over Heart of Midlothian at Dens. Bell scored 10 goals in the nine games and would finish the season as top scorer with 26 goals.

## WEDNESDAY 30th OCTOBER 1990

The Scottish League had introduced a new cup competition for teams outside the top flight to celebrate their centenary and Dundee reach the final of the Centenary Cup with a 2-0 win over Kilmarnock at Rugby Park in the semi-final, thanks to a double from Keith Wright. Wright is inducted into the Dundee Hall of Fame in 2017 with a Legends Award.

## WEDNESDAY 31st OCTOBER 1962

Dundee are roared on by a 32,000 crowd to a 4-1 win over Sporting Clube de Portugal to progress in the European Cup 4-2 on aggregate. Alan Gilzean levels the tie on 13 minutes and right on half time Alan Cousin heads a Gordon Smith cross in off the underside of the bar to put Dundee ahead at a crucial time. Thirty-eight-year-old Smith is at his best and sets up both Dundee's third and fourth goals which are scored by Gilzean to complete his hat-trick. Figuerido pulls one back for the Lisbon side but it doesn't take the shine off a superb performance which has sent the Dark Blues into the last eight of the Champions Cup.

# DUNDEE FC
## *On This Day*

# NOVEMBER

## WEDNESDAY 1st NOVEMBER 1967

Bobby Cox returns to the starting line-up for the Inter-Cities Fairs Cup second round match with Royal Leige at Dens, four days after the League Cup final. Two Alex Stuart 'specials' and a Sammy Wilson header gives The Dee a 3-1 first leg win to take to Belgium.

## MONDAY 1st NOVEMBER 2010

Dundee are deducted 25 points by the Scottish Football League for going into administration for a second time and a ban is imposed on signing any new players. The punishment is a serious threat to the club's very existence and it leaves Dundee on minus 11 points, bottom of the league, 20 points behind the nearest team Greenock Morton and in a state of shock.

## WEDNESDAY 2nd NOVEMBER 1960

Alan Gilzean scores five as Dundee defeat Keith 9-0 at home in a Dewar Shield semi-final; a competition competed for by the winners of the Aberdeenshire, Forfarshire, Perthshire and Stirlingshire Cups. Curlett and Robertson get a brace each to complete the scoring in front of 1,000 fans and they would beat St Johnstone 4-2 in the final at Dens 11 months later.

## WEDNESDAY 3rd NOVEMBER 1971

Dundee look to overturn a 2-1 first leg deficit against Cologne at Dens in the Uefa Cup and John Duncan levels the tie with a header after 12 minutes. However, after 59 minutes The Dee looked out when goals from Simmet and Flohe gave the West Germans a 4-2 aggregate lead. John Duncan pulled one back ten minutes later and the big striker completed his hat-trick with six minutes left to make it 4-4. This would be enough to send the West Germans through on the new away goals rule. Dundee put Cologne under intense pressure and Jim Steele and Duncan have shots cleared off the line before Bobby Wilson crashed home the winner in the dying seconds for a 4-2 win on the night and a 5-4 win on aggregate. *The People's Journal* described it as, 'the greatest game of the century at Dens Park.'

## SATURDAY 4th NOVEMBER 1961

Dundee meet Celtic in their title-winning season at Dens and crowd trouble breaks out both in the ground and in the city centre afterwards, where pubs are closed on the order of the Dundee police. Bobby Wishart gives Dundee an eighth minute lead when he scores from 20 yards out before Carroll equalises before the break. Alan Gilzean heads home the winner on the hour to keep the Dark Blues at the top of the league.

## WEDNESDAY 5th NOVEMBER 1980

Dundee are at Somerset Park for a League Cup semi-final first leg tie with fellow First Division side Ayr United. Several Dundee players are affected by a flu virus with George McGeachie unable to resume after the break but only a last gasp equaliser from future Dee Robert Connor earns Ayr United a draw after Eric Sinclair has given the Dark Blues the lead.

## SATURDAY 5th NOVEMBER 1983

Peter Mackie's 19th-minute goal secures a famous 1-0 win over Dundee United, the Dark Blues first derby win for four years. Mackie latches onto a Cammy Fraser through ball, rounds Hamish McAlpine and slots into the empty net in front of the delirious Dees on the Arklay Street terracing at Tannadice.

## SUNDAY 6th NOVEMBER 1994

Dundee lose the Scottish League Challenge Cup final 3-2 to Airdrieonians at McDiarmid Park in Perth. Paul Harvey puts the Diamonds ahead but The Dee level just before the interval when Graham Hay puts through his own net under pressure from Gerry Britton. In 62 minutes a rash tackle from Paul Tosh allows future Dundee coach Jimmy Boyle to score from the spot but Gerry Britton sends the match into extra time when he rams home a George Shaw cut-back. Nine minutes before penalties Michel Pageaud spills a Graham Harvey shot which allows substitute Andy Smith to crash home the winner and lift the Challenge Cup.

## SATURDAY 6th NOVEMBER 2004

Substitute John Sutton scores five minutes from the end to give The Dee a 1-0 victory over nine-man Dundee United. Dundee manager Jim Duffy is forced pre-match to replace regular goalkeeper Derek Soutar with Kelvin Jack due to illness but the Trinidad and Tobago international limps off with a thigh injury after 30 minutes and is replaced by Soutar. United's Chris Innes is sent off after the break, when he hauls down Steve Lovell on the edge of the box and Mark Wilson follows for a deliberate handball. The Dark Blues struggle against the nine men until United keeper Paul Jarvie allows Sutton's header at the back post to squirm between his legs and into the net.

## SATURDAY 7th NOVEMBER 2009

Future Dee John Baird drives home from 12 yards to give Airdrie United a 25th minute lead at Dens but a Sean Higgins double ensures the Dark Blues side fight back to claim the three points. His first comes three minutes after the Diamonds' opener with the easiest of headers from six yards and the second when the little striker takes advantage of space, slamming the ball home from the middle of the box.

## SATURDAY 8th NOVEMBER 1986

A brace from Graham Harvey and a goal from Rab Shannon secures a 3-0 win over joint league leaders Dundee United at Tannadice. When the Dundee fans pick up the Monday papers to read about the win, they are stunned to learn that Ray Stephen has joined Arsene Wenger's Nancy for £150,000.

## SATURDAY 9th NOVEMBER 2013

Craig Wighton becomes Dundee's youngest ever scorer as The Dee beat Raith Rovers 2-0 at Dens on the way to winning the SPFL Championship. Ryan Conroy gives Dundee a 28th minute lead before 16-year-old Wighton heads home just after the break to create history.

## SATURDAY 10th NOVEMBER 1945

Albert Juliussen scores five as Dundee defeat Arbroath 8-0 at Dens en route to winning the Scottish League B Division title. Willie Anderson, Gerry Follon and Reggie Smith get the other goals and 'Big Julie' would finish the season as top goal scorer with 42 goals.

ALAN GILZEAN HEADS HOME DUNDEE'S FIRST IN THE 5-1 WIN OVER RANGERS AT IBROX

## SATURDAY 11th NOVEMBER 1961

Dundee produce their greatest ever League result with a 5-1 win at Rangers on the way to winning the title. Swirling fog makes visibility very poor and police turn back many Dundee buses, saying that the game is off. Those who are in Ibrox aren't sure how many Dundee score in the second half after the first half finishes 0-0. Scot Symon's men can't cope with Alan Gilzean in the air with the Dundee number 10 scoring an incredible four goals. Gillie opens the scoring in 47 minutes when he heads past Billy Ritchie and a minute later adds a second but the fog is so bad that Dundee keeper Pat Liney doesn't know Dundee are two up until skipper Bobby Cox informs him. Gilzean completes his hat-trick on 74 minutes before Ralph Brand pulls one back for the hosts. Gilzean scores his fourth on 87 minutes and Andy Penman makes it five 60 seconds later to obliterate Rangers' unbeaten record in all competitions and move Dundee seven points clear at the top of Division One.

## SUNDAY 11th NOVEMBER 1990

Dundee win the Scottish League Centenary Cup thanks to a Billy Dodds hat-trick in a 3-2 win over Ayr United at Fir Park. Ayr take the lead on 13 minutes but with Colin West causing havoc out wide, Dodds equalises from the spot after the winger is downed just after the break. Twenty minutes later the wee striker puts Dundee in front from an inch perfect cross from West but David Smyth's shot is deflected high past Tom Carson to make it 2-2. With five minutes left Purdie makes a brave save at the feet of Keith Wright but Dodds is on hand to score and win Dundee's first knock-out trophy since 1973.

## SATURDAY 11th NOVEMBER 2000

Dundee walked down Tannadice Street and record their second derby win of the season. With half time approaching Willie Falconer cleverly plays in Claudio Caniggia and the Argentinian speeds through to pick his spot in the net. Dundee have to wait until the 73rd minute for their second and it is scored in sensational style after a rapier like move. Controlling a pass from Barry Smith, Caniggia back-heels to Giorgi Nemsadze and the Georgian ghosts past two Dundee United defenders before brilliantly chipping the ball up and over the helpless Alan Combe to secure the 2-0 win.

## SATURDAY 12th NOVEMBER 1927

Dundee record their biggest win of the season as Gus Smith scores a hat-trick in a 7-0 win over Kilmarnock at Dens. Smith would finish as top scorer at the end of the season with 24 goals and again the following year with 15.

## SATURDAY 13th NOVEMBER 1971

Dundee defeat Rangers 3-2 at Ibrox thanks to goals from Alex Kinninmouth, Gordon Wallace and Dave Johnston. Dundee would do the league double over Rangers with a 2-0 win at Dens in April.

## SATURDAY 13th NOVEMBER 2010

Dundee travel to the Highlands to face Ross County with the club in administration and large sections of the Dark Blue support claim they want to boycott away matches and instead donate the money they would have spent directly to the club. The club therefore open the Penman Lounge at Dens and whilst raising some much needed cash, the Dees who don't travel to the Highlands must have a tinge of regret when news of Dundee's first away win of the season comes filtering through on *Soccer Saturday*. It is an excellent performance by all accounts as Leigh Griffiths inspires Dundee to a 3-0 win, scoring a double himself and setting up Nicky Riley for a goal between his strikes.

## SATURDAY 14th NOVEMBER 1964

Goals from Andy Penman and Steve Murray give Dundee a 2-0 win over Celtic at Parkhead, their first win at Celtic Park for five years in any competition.

## WEDNESDAY 15th NOVEMBER 1967

George McLean sets a new club record of most goals in a European match. Dundee travel to Belgium to face Royal Liege in the Inter-Cities Fairs Cup second round second leg and McLean scores all four for a dynamic Dark Blues as they win 4-1 to progress 7-2 on aggregate. In the Stade Vélodrome de Rocourt away dressing room McLean quips to his manager, 'You'd better take the number off my jersey Mr Ancell, and replace it with an S for Superman.'

## SATURDAY 16th NOVEMBER 1991

After a double on his debut in a 3-1 win at Hamilton the week before, Eddie Gallagher scores a hat-trick as Dundee beat promotion rivals Partick Thistle 6-2 at Firhill. Kevin Bremner also nets a brace and his second, a bullet header from a John McQuillan cross (who gets the sixth), is voted European goal of the week on the fledgling Sky Sports.

## SATURDAY 17th NOVEMBER 1934

Dundee defeat Partick Thistle 4-1 at Firhill with a brace each from Gibby McNaughton and Archie Coats. Coats is the club's second top scorer of all time behind Alan Gilzean, with 158 goals in 234 appearances.

## SATURDAY 18th NOVEMBER 1961

Raith Rovers come across the Tay by train and are ahead 1-0 at the break before two headers in two minutes from Alan Gilzean gives the white-shirted Dee the lead. However, with just 20 minutes left, Rovers are 4-2 in front after scoring three times in a mad five minutes. Bobby Wishart pulls a goal back with an unstoppable shot and with four minutes left Bobby Seith uncorks another rocket to equalise. Then, in the dying seconds, Gordon Smith fires home from just inside the box to win the game 5-4 and is mobbed by his teammates as fans invade the pitch in celebration. Bobby Seith describes the match as a 'key moment' in the title winning year and says, 'Dundee's never-say-die attitude, allied with our undoubted skill, was able to rescue a victory from the jaws of defeat.'

## WEDNESDAY 18th NOVEMBER 1964

After getting a bye in the first round, European football returns to Dens when Real Zaragoza arrive for a European Cup Winners Cup second round first leg match. Dundee have qualified after losing to league champions Rangers in the Scottish Cup final in April. Steve Murray heads Dundee in front early on, only for the Spaniards to reply with a lightning double midway in the first half but Doug Houston rescues a draw with two minutes remaining.

## SATURDAY 18th NOVEMBER 1995

Dundee prepare for a League Cup final by crossing Tannadice Street for a First Division derby with Dundee United. Two quickfire headed goals from George Shaw give the Dark Blues a comfortable half time lead and just after the break, a Morten Weighorst header makes it 3-0. Goals by Brewster and Malpas make it a nervy end for The Dee but they hang on for an enjoyable 3-2 win. The Dundee fans sing 'We're going to Hampden' at the final whistle and enjoy the victory again on *Sportscene* at night.

## WEDNESDAY 19th NOVEMBER 1980

Dundee beat Ayr United 3-2 at Dens in the League Cup semi-final second leg to progress to the final 4-3 on aggregate. There is a certain eeriness about Dens with the South Enclosure closed for the installation of bench seating but, on a rain soaked pitch, Billy Williamson gives Dundee a 22nd minute lead. Gerry Christie equalises for the Honest Men but before the break, Dundee skipper Stewart MacLaren is stretchered off and would miss the final. Billy McColl puts Ayr ahead after an hour but Cammy Fraser bursts through to level before Eric Sinclair crashes home a winner near the end to send the home fans wild with delight.

## SATURDAY 20th NOVEMBER 1948

Dundee lose 4-1 to Rangers in a controversial League Cup semi-final, played in gale force wind and rain at Hampden. Rangers skipper Jock Shaw wins the toss and chooses to play with the elements but the referee allows them to also kick off when Dundee should have started the game. Rangers are 3-0 up after seven minutes and score a fourth in 25 against ten-man Dundee who lose centre-half Tommy Gray after just two minutes when he is injured trying to prevent the opening goal. A late Reggie Smith penalty is scant consolation.

## SATURDAY 21st NOVEMBER 1925

A crowd of 18,000 turn out at Dens Park for the first ever top flight derby between Dundee and Dundee United who changed their name from Dundee Hibernian in 1923. The usually reliable David 'Napper' Thomson misses a penalty and the match ends 0-0.

## WEDNESDAY 21st NOVEMBER 1973

Goals from Jimmy Wilson and Gordon Wallace earn Dundee a 2-2 draw with Clyde at Shawfield in the League Cup quarter-final second leg. With a John Duncan goal giving the Dark Blues a 1-0 win at Dens on Halloween in the 1st leg, The Dee go through 3-2 on aggregate.

## SUNDAY 22nd NOVEMBER 1998

Dundee United claim it's the 100th league derby, conveniently forgetting the 1917/18 matches as Dundee Hibernian, and it takes some inspired defending at Tannadice to keep the home side at bay. With 20 minutes left James Grady comes on for Tommy Coyne and on 82 minutes he runs on to an Eddie Annand head flick and volleys a spectacular 18-yarder into the roof of the net. It still takes a superb save from Robert Douglas to secure the 1-0 win before he has to tackle a United fan who has run on to the pitch to attack him at the final whistle. The Grady goal is inducted into the club's Hall of Fame in 2015 with a Modern Moment Award and the match ball now resides in the Dens Park boardroom. Robert Douglas is inducted into the club's Hall of Fame in 2017 with a Modern Heroes Award.

## SUNDAY 22nd NOVEMBER 2009

Dundee came back from two goals down to win the Scottish League Challenge Cup 3-2 with victory over Inverness Caledonian Thistle at McDiarmid Park. Adam Rooney heads the Highlanders into a 20th-minute lead and Nauris Bulvitis grabs Inverness' second before half-time but scores an own goal early in the second period to give Dundee a route back into the game. Gary Harkins equalised with a close-range strike and then sets up Craig Forsyth to grab a late winner. It is Dundee's second Challenge Cup win and Jocky Scott becomes the first manager to win all three cup competitions in Scotland, having been co-manager of Aberdeen when they won the League Cup and Scottish Cup in season 1989/90. Colin Cameron also becomes the first player to win the Football League trophy north and south of the border.

DUNDEE CELEBRATE THEIR 2009 SCOTTISH LEAGUE CHALLENGE CUP WIN AT McDIARMID PARK

## SATURDAY 23rd NOVEMBER 1985

Ten-man Dundee record a sensational 3-2 win over Rangers thanks to a John Brown hat-trick. Tosh McKinlay is sent off on 17 minutes with the scores at 0-0 after a crude challenge on Ted McMinn. Bomber's first saw him leave a trail of Rangers' defenders in his wake, his second a fantastic free kick and the third a penalty to give the Dark Blues their fourth successive win in a six-game unbeaten sequence against the Light Blues.

## SATURDAY 23rd NOVEMBER 2002

Dundee are magnificent for the first hour of a derby against Dundee United at Dens and race into a 3-0 lead. A brilliant run and cross by Nacho Novo allows Fabian Caballero to open the scoring with a downward header and the Argentinian makes it 2-0 when his shot deflects off Steve Lovell's back and into the net. Venezuelan full-back Jonny Hernandez makes it three soon after half-time but United hit back twice through Jim Hamilton and Jim McIntyre. Ex-Dee Hamilton misses an easy header in injury time and the match ends 3-2 to The Dee.

## WEDNESDAY 24th NOVEMBER 1971

Dundee meet old European Cup foes AC Milan in the Uefa Cup third round first leg in the San Siro. Dundee adopt a defensive formation with Iain Phillip playing as a sweeper behind the back four but lose an early goal to Italian 'Golden Boy' Gianni Rivera. Shortly after half-time a misunderstanding between George Stewart and Ally Donaldson sees the defender send the ball into the empty net before a third from Romeo Benetti gives Dundee an uphill task for the second leg.

## SATURDAY 25th NOVEMBER 1950

George Christie and Johnny Pattillo each score a brace and Doug Cowie a penalty as Dundee defeat Partick Thistle 5-0 in front of a 20,000 crowd at Dens. Cowie would finish as that season's top scorer with just eight goals, six of which are penalties.

## SUNDAY 26th NOVEMBER 1995

It's a desperately disappointing day for the 16,000 Dees at Hampden as First Division Dundee lose 2-0 to Aberdeen in the League Cup final. 'For whatever reason too many players did not perform,' says manager Jim Duffy as the Dark Blues fail to show their flair of recent weeks. Goals from Duncan Shearer and ex-Dee Billy Dodds either side of half-time take the cup back to Pittodrie.

## SATURDAY 27th NOVEMBER 1982

Dundee run riot at home as they demolish Kilmarnock 5-2 at Dens Park in front of 4,311 spectators in the Premier Division. The Dark Blues' goals that day come from Cammy Fraser, Jimmy Murphy (2), Davie Bell and Peter Mackie.

## SATURDAY 28th NOVEMBER 1987

Tommy Coyne goes back across the road to haunt his former club with two opportunist goals against Dundee United at Tannadice, set up by the foraging Keith Wright. Wright himself adds a third late on to secure the 3-1 win after Stuart Rafferty's long range shot rebounds off the post as the Dundee fans taunt the Arabs by singing, 'Thank you very much for Tommy Coyne' to the tune of the Cadbury's Roses television advert that aired at the time.

## SUNDAY 28th NOVEMBER 1999

Dundee secure their best result of the season with a 2-1 win over Rangers at Ibrox. Craig Ireland puts them ahead with a powerful header from a Shaun McSkimming corner on 14 minutes and although Robert Douglas saves a Jorg Albertz penalty, Rangers later equalise through Rod Wallace. However, Dundee are not to be denied and deep into injury time Steven Boyack cleverly cushions a Hugh Robertson crossfield pass and the oncoming Gavin Rae celebrates his 22nd birthday by firing home the winner.

## WEDNESDAY 29th NOVEMBER 1961

For the only time in the 20th century, three Dundee players line up in the same Scotland side when Alex Hamilton, Ian Ure and Hugh Robertson face Czechoslovakia in a World Cup play-off match in the Heysel Stadium in Brussels. Hamilton would win 24 Scotland caps and Ian Ure 11 while at Dens but the 4-2 extra time defeat to the Czechs is Robertson's only cap.

## SATURDAY 30th NOVEMBER

Dundee win the Forfarshire Cup with a 2-0 win over Dundee United at Tannadice thanks to goals from Ross Jack and John Brown. It is the first time the Dark Blues have won the local cup competition since 1970/71; a competition The Dee have won 28 times in their history.

# DUNDEE FC
## *On This Day*

# DECEMBER

## SATURDAY 1st DECEMBER 1962

Alan Gilzean equals Albert Juliussen's 1947 club record of most goals scored in a game when he nets seven as Dundee beat Queen of the South 10-2 at Dens. Queens' keeper George Farm is stretchered off in 12 minutes with the score at 2-1 to Dundee after colliding with Gilzean, whose six first -half goals is a Scottish record. Gilzean and Juliussen however are one short of Jimmy McGrory's Scottish record of eight in one match that he scored for Celtic in 1928.

## WEDNESDAY 2nd DECEMBER 1992

Morten Weighorst makes his debut as 10-man Dundee come back from 4-2 down to draw 4-4 at St Johnstone. Having lost an early goal, Dundee's problems are exacerbated when goalkeeper Paul Mathers is dismissed for bringing down Paul Wright just outside the box. Steve Pitmann equalises and soon after the break the Dane announces his arrival when he ghosts past three Saints on the edge of the box before firing home. Stand-in keeper Duncan Campbell then concedes three goals in 20 minutes but in an incredible fighting finish, Billy Dodds nets twice to salvage a draw.

## MONDAY 3rd DECEMBER 1973

In a rearranged League Cup semi-final against Kilmarnock, Tommy Gemmell is the hero at both ends as he scores the winner ten minutes after the break and heads two net-bound shots off the line towards the end. Due to the national energy crisis the floodlights are powered by a generator producing only a third of the normal power but the 4,682 crowd just about see Dundee reach their first League Cup final in 21 years.

## WEDNESDAY 3rd DECEMBER 2003

On an emotional night at Dens, Dundee faced Heart of Midlothian in a League Cup quarter-final in the first home game after going into administration. The Dundee Supporters Association launches the Dee4Life Campaign and have collection buckets at the turnstiles before an enthralling night. Lifted by a noisy home support, the Dark Blues take the game to Hearts but the sides are not separated until extra time when, in the 107th minute, local boy Bobby Linn pounces to hit home the winner after Nacho Novo's shot rebounds off the post.

## SATURDAY 4th DECEMBER 1971

Dundee enjoy the perfect build-up for the forthcoming Uefa Cup visit of AC Milan when a Jocky Scott hat-trick and a John Duncan goal gives them a 4-1 win over Airdrieonians in front of 5,000 at Dens Park.

## SATURDAY 5th DECEMBER 1964

The King of Dens Park Alan Gilzean signs off his Dundee career in typical fashion with a brilliant hat-trick in a 4-4 home draw with St Johnstone. It is Gillie's last game for The Dee as 11 days later he signs for Tottenham Hotspur for a new Scottish record fee of £72,500. The Dundee board are quick to try and appease the fans by splashing out a new record fee between two Scottish clubs of £40,000 to Aberdeen for Charlie Cooke.

## SATURDAY 6th DECEMBER 1980

Dundee meet Dundee United in an historic League Cup final at Dens; the venue decided by the toss of a coin. Eric Sinclair heads the ball into the net after Hamish McAlpine fumbles a high cross from Eric Schaedler but city referee Bob Valentine rules that the keeper has been fouled. Valentine would later deny the Dark Blues a penalty when McAlpine sends Ray Stephen sprawling, but by then United are 2-0 ahead through Davie Dodds and Paul Sturrock. United are too strong for their First Division hosts and Sturrock adds a third seven minutes from time to take the trophy back across the road for the second season in a row.

## SATURDAY 7th DECEMBER 1901

Dundee defeat Heart of Midlothian 2-0 at Dens with goals from Tommy Robertson and David Mackay. Dundee would finish second bottom but are saved from having to seek re-election when the ten-team Scottish League Division One is increased to 12 clubs the following year.

## TUESDAY 8th DECEMBER 1964

Dundee lose 2-1 away at Real Zaragoza in the European Cup Winners Cup and go out 4-3 on aggregate. Hugh Robertson gives Dundee an early lead but two goals from international winger Carlos

Laperta just before half-time puts the Spaniards ahead in the tie. With Bobby Cox hirpling on the wing in the second half after pulling a muscle, Dundee are unable to recover the deficit and bow out in their only ever entry into the Cup Winners' Cup.

## WEDNESDAY 8th DECEMBER 1971

AC Milan come to Dens defending a 3-0 first leg lead in the third round of the Uefa Cup. A grimly determined Dundee besieged the Italians' goalmouth and get their reward on 38 minutes when Gordon Wallace heads a Duncan Lambie cross past Cudicini. After the break, Dundee's pressure continues with the Serie A side wasting time at every opportunity. With 16 minutes left, the superb Lambie rattles a 30-yard shot off the post and John Duncan is on the spot to score. Urged on by a 15,500 crowd, Dundee desperately try to take the game into extra time but to no avail, but the exhilarating performance is given a standing ovation at the end.

## FRIDAY 8th DECEMBER 1995

Barry Smith signs for Dundee as part of the deal which takes Morten Weighorst to Celtic and becomes a Dundee great, making 433 appearances over the next 11 years. Smith wins the Dundee Player of the Year in 1997, his first as captain and leads the Dark Blues out in the 2003 Scottish Cup final and into premier European competition for the first time in 29 years. He is inducted into the inaugural Hall of Fame in 2009 and the following year takes over as manager when the club goes into administration. After being deducted 25 points by the Scottish League, Smith leads them to safety in the incredible Dee-Fiant season. The achievement is recognised by League sponsors Irn-Bru who present Smith with the Phenomenal Achievement of the Season Award. A true Dundee legend.

## SATURDAY 9th DECEMBER 1916

Davie Brown scores all six as Dundee beat Raith Rovers 6-2 in the Scottish League Division One match at Dens. With the country in the midst of war only 2,000 turn up to witness the first double hat-trick in the club's history.

## SATURDAY 10th DECEMBER 1910

A brace each from Jimmy Bellamy and RC Hamilton earn Dundee a 4-1 win over Heart of Midlothian at Dens. Scottish internationalist Hamilton would finish his inaugural Dark Blue season as top scorer with 20 goals.

## SATURDAY 11th DECEMBER 1993

Rugged centre-half Noel Blake makes his debut after signing from Bradford City for £15,000 and a goal from Croatian Dragutin Ristic earns Dundee a 1-1 draw with Celtic at Dens Park.

## SATURDAY 12th DECEMBER 1987

A brace each from Tommy Coyne and Keith Wright and two own goals from future Dee Roddy Manley gives Dundee a 6-0 win over Falkirk at Brockville. Centre-half Manley joins Dundee in 1995 and would turn out for The Dee in the League Cup final against Aberdeen but those two goals would be his only two goals for the Dark Blues.

## SATURDAY 13th DECEMBER 1986

Tommy Coyne makes his debut against St Mirren at Dens after joining from Dundee United for £70,000. However, it is two goals each from Keith Wright and Graham Harvey and a goal and a penalty from John Brown and Jim Duffy respectively, which earns the 6-3 win.

## TUESDAY 14th DECEMBER 2010

Dundee fan Leighton McIntosh achieves his ambition of playing at Dens Park when he comes off the bench for Leigh Griffiths in the 3-0 home win over Cowdenbeath. The victory in the rearranged fixture means that administration-ravaged Dundee are now eight games undefeated and, for many, the win is redemption for the terrible defeat to the Fife side in September. The Blue Brazil had been the last team to beat Dundee but goals from Craig Forsyth, Nicky Riley and Craig McKeown, his first for the club, ensure that there is no repeat.

## SATURDAY 15th DECEMBER 1973

For days before the League Cup final against Celtic at Hampden blizzards all over Scotland cast doubts over the game right up to the 1.30pm kick off, brought forward to avoid using the floodlights during the national energy crisis. Conditions are appalling throughout the game with sleet and snow turning to driving rain and the attendance of 29,974 is the lowest ever for a League Cup final. Chances are few and far between but with 14 minutes remaining Bobby Wilson is fouled on the halfway line by Paul Wilson. The full-back, inducted into Dundee's Hall of Fame in 2013, takes the free kick himself and sends it curving towards Gordon Wallace inside the Celtic box. With his back to goal, Wallace takes the ball on his chest and in one movement turns and sweeps a low shot into the net to win the League Cup for Dundee.

## SATURDAY 16th DECEMBER 1961

Dundee face Airdrieonians at Dens in their championship-winning season. Gordon Smith moves to centre-forward after Alan Gilzean unknowingly breaks his jaw in the 2-2 draw at Stirling Albion in the previous match. Bobby Wishart opens the scoring on three minutes but Airdrie hit the post before Smith doubles the lead nine minutes after the break. Alan Cousin scores a third after a one-two with Hugh Robertson before twice returning the favour for Shug to score, as Dundee win 5-1.

## WEDNESDAY 16th DECEMBER 1987

Four days after scoring six at Falkirk, Dundee win 7-1 at Morton. The Cobra and the Mongoose make it nine goals in four days for the deadly duo as Tommy Coyne scores a hat-trick and Keith Wright two. George 'Zico' McGeachie and Graham Harvey complete the rout. It is the last time Dundee score five or more away from home in the top flight until a 5-1 win at Fir Park against Motherwell on February 25th 2017 when all five goals were scored in the first half.

## SATURDAY 17th DECEMBER 1898

On the same day the Dark Blues go down 7-0 to Rangers at Ibrox, the Dundee Football and Athletic Club are placed into voluntary liquidation after a shareholders meeting is held in the Royal British

Hotel where they are told that the debts are £400 and the assets, apart from the stands, are virtually nil. However, this is not done until a deal is struck between the new owners (Messrs Anderson and Cameron who step forward from the old committee to run the club) and the receivers, where crucially it is agreed that the players and the stands would remain with the club. The Scottish Football League are delighted that its northern-most club has survived and it waives their right to the players' registrations and while it could be said that this is a new Dundee, this time called just plain Dundee Football Club, it is also agreed by the League that this new entity is considered the same team and would fulfill Dundee's fixtures. Three days later a new committee is formed at a packed public meeting at Gilfillan Hall.

## TUESDAY 17th DECEMBER 1996

Lee Power makes his debut after joining on a free from Peterborough United as Dundee defeat East Fife 7-1 at Bayview. Fourteen days previously the match in Methil is abandoned at half-time after the floodlights fail in the gale force winds with Dundee 2-1 ahead. The goals from O'Driscoll and Raeside are Dundee's first in six games but in the rearranged game The Dee demolish the Fifers with goals from David Winnie, Jerry O'Driscoll, Gavin Rae, Iain Anderson (2), Robbie Raeside and Paul Tosh.

## SATURDAY 18th DECEMBER 2004

Dundee are now six games unbeaten against Aberdeen after a Neil Barrett goal is enough to give the Dark Blues a 1-0 win over The Dons at Dens. Future Dee Steven Craig comes off the bench for the Reds in the first half only to be sent off in 67 minutes.

## SATURDAY 19th DECEMBER 1931

A Davie Balfour hat-trick helps Dundee earn a 4-2 win over Rangers in front of 16,000 at Dens to gain revenge for the opening day 4-1 defeat at Ibrox. Balfour is that season's top scorer with 22 goals while Harry Smith nets Dundee's other counter.

## SATURDAY 20th DECEMBER 1997

Dundee win 2-0 at St Mirren on the way to winning the First Division thanks to goals from Iain Anderson and Paisley-born James Grady. The Dark Blues concede just 24 goals on the way to winning promotion and keep 17 cleans sheets which undoubtedly helps goalkeeper Robert Douglas win the first of his three Dundee Player of the Year awards at the end of the season.

## SATURDAY 21st DECEMBER 2013

Peter MacDonald's second half goal gives Dundee victory at Paul Hartley's Alloa Athletic and moves John Brown's side to the top of the Scottish Championship. MacDonald gets on the end of Martin Boyle's cross to head home before Iain Davidson sees red for violent conduct in injury time.

## SATURDAY 22nd DECEMBER 1923

Season 1923/24 sees Davie Halliday and Davie McLean develop a potent striking partnership and both are on target as Dundee defeat Celtic 2-1 at Dens. McLean's experience brings out the best in Halliday who rattles in 39 goals, one more than his total for the previous two seasons combined. Thirty-eight are scored in the league, a tally that remains a Dens Park record to this day.

## SATURDAY 23rd DECEMBER 2000

A steel band provides plenty of background rhythm for the 9,093 crowd for the visit of Aberdeen to Dens and goals by Argentinians Beto Carranza and Juan Sara give Dundee a 2-1 lead after an hour. However, the game ends in controversy when Aberdeen referee Alan Freeland first denies Claudio Caniggia a clear penalty, then awards a soft one to The Dons for a push by Barry Smith. Arild Stavrum equalises from the spot and, at the full time whistle, Caniggia receives a second yellow for dissent. Manager Ivano Bonetti is apoplectic post-match and complains to the press, 'In Italy when you play Roma, you do not get a referee from Rome!'

## SATURDAY 24th DECEMBER 1949

A healthy Christmas Eve crowd of 13,000 witnesses Dundee defeat Stirling Albion 4-1 at Dens thanks to goals from Jimmy Toner (2),

George Stewart and Syd Gerrie. Toner would play in both the 1951 and 1952 League Cup wins and is inducted into the club's Hall of Fame in 2016 with a Golden Era Award.

## SATURDAY 25th DECEMBER 1976

The last Christmas Day match at Dens sees Dundee defeat Montrose 1-0 in the Scottish League First Division. Just 3,500 turn up at Dens to see Ian Purdie score the winner in the Dark Blues' eighth game without loss.

## TUESDAY 26th DECEMBER 2000

Despite Claudio Caniggia being suspended for the trip to Fir Park after being sent off after full-time three days before, Dundee defeat Motherwell 3-0. On a freezing, foggy Boxing Day, a double from Juan Sara and a strike from Gavin Rae secures the three points.

## TUESDAY 27th DECEMBER 1969

Dundee continued their good form at home with a 1-0 win over high-flying Hibernian. The winner comes from Doug Houston, the only Dee to play in two European semi-finals for the club, to give the Dark Blues five wins and a draw at Dens since October.

## SATURDAY 28th DECEMBER 1996

Eleven days after putting seven past East Fife at Bayview Dundee defeat East Fife 6-0 at Dens thanks to goals from Paul Tosh (2), Lee Power, Chic Charnley and Jerry O'Driscoll (2), who would finish the season as top scorer.

## SATURDAY 29th DECEMBER 1917

Dundee score 11 goals for the first time in their history in an 11-2 win over Dunfermline to win the Loftus Cup. The Loftus Cup is an invitational competition for teams in the east and central area and is the brainchild of Dundee Hibernian founder Pat Riley. The trophy is donated by famous Dundee baker David Wallace and named after his residence, Loftus House in Broughty Ferry. In the absence of the Scottish and Forfarshire Cups during World War One Dundee enter and win the Penman Cup and the Loftus Cup as well as the Scottish League Eastern Division.

## SATURDAY 30th DECEMBER 1950

Dundee are the first team in Scotland to wear Continental rubber boots to combat the frosty and heavily-sanded pitch at Dens and goals from Ally Gunn and Ernie Ewen give them a 2-0 win over Rangers in front of 37,400.

## SATURDAY 31st DECEMBER 1988

On Hogmanay Dave Smith's struggling Dark Blues record their first home win over Aberdeen since 1975 with a well-merited 2-0 win against The Dons. Dundee are reputed to be on their biggest ever win bonus and play with a passion rarely displayed that season as a Tommy Coyne double secures the win. Just one point from the next three games sees Smith resign in January after just five wins in his seven months in charge – two of which are against Celtic!

TOMMY COYNE SLOTS THE BALL PAST THEO SNELDERS IN THE ABERDEEN GOAL IN A FAMOUS HOGMANAY WIN